The Political Key to the Republican Tarot

Wizard Design
http://awizardslife.com
Austin, Texas

ISBN 978-1-4357-0113-7

© M. G. WIZARD, 2007 ♠
published by Lulu
www.lulu.com

The Political Key to the

Republican Tarot

Being Fragments of a Secret Tradition
Under the Veil of Representative Government

by Mariann G. Wizard

With 79 plates, illustrating the Greater and Lesser Arcana,
and a Joker

♥

For Friends of Forty+ Years:
Kate for Time & the Tarts,
Robert for the Knaves,
Liz for Strength,
Marilyn for Pineapple Surprises;
for Terry, who Egged me On,
and Linda, who Laughed out Loud,
and in whose House it was Hatched:
Now may Dame Fortune Smile!

♦

*Passing through the nexus of
West 22nd & Longview Sts.,
not even the Gypsy Witch
could foretell this funny future!*

♣

Preface & Acknowledgments

"The evil that men do lives after them; the good is oft interred with their bones."[i]

I am deeply indebted to **The Pictorial Key to the Tarot**,[ii] the classic tarot reader by Arthur Edward Waite, and to the **Rider-Waite Tarot** deck, designed by Pamela Colman Smith; not only for the wide recognition which makes satire possible; but for insights gleaned over the years from a gifted interpreter of Waite's work. Indeed, although I count myself a skeptic, Waite's archetypes continually amazed me once I conceived the wacky notion of a **Republican Tarot** featuring the ridiculous actors and devolving institutions of the United States of America in the early Third Millennium. Divinatory meanings ascribed to Smith's 78 lavish picture cards in 1910 fairly leapt off Waite's pages to crack my jokes! Let me be clear at the outset that my intention in devising this work is frankly mercantile and farcical, and it should absolutely be used for entertainment purposes only, as should any work which delves into "fortune-telling" (and on that, I believe Waite would agree).

Taking Waite at his word (and his words for all they are worth), I made numerous unauthorized, unjustified, and completely arbitrary changes in the cards, the result of personal "divinations" for fun, satire and profit. These deviations in symbolism, illustration, description, purported meaning and overall craftsmanship are legion. I have received some misguided encouragement, or "egging on", in this misbegotten endeavor, from friends who should be more mature by now, but all deficiencies and *egg*-regious errors are mine alone. The personages who enliven my cards, like the images subverted from Waite's **Tarot** and other mystical sources, such as the public domain, and all new and dubious meanings pasted onto the old, are products of my own warped imagination, and surely not as I've portrayed them. It's the price of fame, Dear Reader; as David Koresh said, *"If you can't stand the heat, don't dial 9-1-1!"*

The problem arose that I am no artist; nor would any of my gifted acquaintances be persuaded to embark on the likely all-but-thankless task of transforming the admirable Ms. Smith's works into images suitable for my perverse political theme. Yet illustration was certainly necessary, and having ascertained that outsourcing the work to India or Japan was also impractical, I resorted to those twin refuges of hacks and scoundrels, clip art and the Internet. Among the former, the observant of a certain age and taste will discern some few of the inimitable characters of *MAD Mgazine*'s **Don Martin**. I am pleased to pay homage here, for Martin and other *MAD*men shaped my own taste in humor, and aversion to hypocrisy, more than some might willingly admit; as did the brazen brigands and adventurers of the latter-day *Texas Ranger*. Nevertheless, the images in **The Republican Tarot** were created by me, on an obsolete computer in a discontinued software program, and thence manipulated unmercifully, within the limits of my capabilities, into their present form. Illustrations of some styles of tarot cards past and present, and campaign buttons supporting typical Republican candidates of the past, are collages of images available from Public Domain Clip Art and similar sources, as are the various Elephants encountered herein.

Arthur Edward Waite attempted, in his lyrical, meditative, and deeply impenetrable work, to steer frivolous "fortune seekers" to more profound paths of self-discovery and inner realization. I, on the other hand, would be happy to steer pompous political wannabes to rewarding new careers in food service, but gladly welcome the most frivolous apolitical "Inquirer" to my scavenger hunt of US history, rumor, and current affairs, where the prizes are, I hope, a few knowingly wicked laughs and modest insights into political games of skill and chance. I offer the small consolation, to those who seek more tangible rewards, that perfectly satisfactory predictions, or "fortunes", may indeed be "read" (and, I hope, *made*), using the cards of the **Republican Tarot**!

Today's political crises are tomorrow's ancient history. If our egotistical movers and shakers would but relax and take a long, contemplative look at their own small importance from time to time, we should all be less subjected to the slings and arrows of their outrageous decisions. The **Tarot**'s message to career politicians and crusading political aspirants alike is: "*Look around, buddy! If you're an archetype a hundred years from now, it's **probably** because you made some **pretty bad choices**! Slow down! Take your time in reinventing government; if it ain't broke, don't fix it!*" As for the cards, Stuart Kaplan writes, "[A]fter you spread the tarot pack you will know what the cards say to you."[iii] *Read 'em and weep*!

I am again indebted to Kate Braun for her comments on this project in draft form, as for so much tarot lore, most generously shared!

Mariann G. Wizard
Conceived Aug 7, 1995, Portland, Oregon, Cascadia
Completed October 10, 2007, Austin, Tejas, Aztlan

The Contents

	PAGE
PREFACE & ACKNOWLEDGMENTS	v

An expression of personal indebtedness -- My mercantile *and* farcical intent -- New careers in customer service -- *"If it ain't broke, don't fix it."*.

ILLUSTRATION: Some Tarot styles of the past and present. . . . . *viii*

PART I
THE PARTY AND ITS SYMBOLS
- § 1. - Introductory *and* General. 1

ILLUSTRATION: An ancestral Republican? 4
- § 2. - Class I. The Trumps Major, otherwise Greater Arcana. 5
- § 3. - Class II. The Four Suites, otherwise Lesser Arcana. 9
- § 4. - The Tarot in History. 11
- § 5. - The Republican Party in History. 12

PART II
THE DOCTRINE BEHIND THE PARTY
- § 1. - The Party *and* Secret Tradition. 18

ILLUSTRATION: Some candidates of the past 21
- § 2. - The Trumps Major *and* their Inner Symbolism 22
- § 3. - The Greater Arcana *and* Their Divinatory Meanings 69

PART III
THE OUTER METHOD OF THE ORACLES
- § 1. - Distinction between the Greater *and* Lesser Arcana. 72
- § 2. - The Lesser Arcana, otherwise, the *Four Suites of Tarot Cards* 73
  - The Suite of Bushes.
  - The Suite of Pineapples.
  - The Suite of Arms.
  - The Suite of Coins.
- § 3. – Conclusion as to the Greater Keys 200
- § 4. – A Note on The Joker 203
- § 5. – The Art of Tarot Divination. 205
- § 6. – An Ancient Celtic Method of Divination. 206
- § 7. – The Politics as Life ("Triple-Cross") Method of Reading the Tarot Cards. 207

ILLUSTRATION: Many reside within the Big Tent. 209

AFTERWORD: CONFESSION 208
BIBLIOGRAPHIC NOTE 210
ENDNOTES 211

Some Tarot styles of the past and present.

PART I
The Party and its Symbols

§ I
INTRODUCTORY AND GENERAL.

While there is no shortage of silliness in political life today; still the question remains as to whether or not this silliness is pathological. While I do not think that there is a pathology dedicated to politics, about various public extravagances no one can question their derangement, and if anyone does, you have only to show him or her this present volume to set aside all doubt. Such pathology, if it existed, would no doubt have no reputable treatment, but be the province of quacks and fakirs. Now, *Magick* is not unlike Politics, though it seldom works in accord with it in everyday life. And we should not fall prey to the notion that simply because a thing is unlikely, it has no other, for instance, amusement, value. After long dealing with dubious dignitaries and sham solemnities, it is always refreshing, in the realm of the arts, to encounter that which is obviously fraudulent, or at least completely absurd! So it is with the **Republican Tarot!**

While the organization of this study may make very little sense to you, or to me, for that matter, it is intended to closely mimic Arthur Edward Waite's grandiose and mystifying scheme of things, which seems a blueprint for what he calls "lacerations... inflict[ed] on the logical understanding." And this is as it should be, for while an understanding of party politics, on the highest plane, is a key to Mysteries, of which "the wrong symbolical stories have been told... and the wrong history has been given in every published work which so far has dealt with the subject", and again, as regards the Secret Tradition, "there is always the possibility that some minor arcana... may be made public with a flourish of trumpets"[iv] [yet] "any revelation will contain only a third part of the [facts, so that] the guardians of certain temples of initiation[v] who keep watch over mysteries of this order have therefore no cause for alarm."

Or, to speak plainly for once, the general public is not intended to see how it is regularly sheared; nor do many wish to observe the process of sausage-making.

In my preface to **The Republican Tarot**, which, rather by accident, has come to be completed after a long period of lying fallow, I have said what was possible or seemed most necessary. The present work is designed more especially – as I have intimated – to introduce a new Tarot deck and to pamper myself with the ill-gotten gains, so far as this is possible without attracting the attention of the taxing authorities!

Here is a hint for those who seek to understand the **Republican Tarot**: not all answers are given within, neither in the endnotes, nor in the bibliography; yet even the most obscure references may be followed by those who but apply themselves to observing what is here portrayed, in many instances, as the Circus of Political Life. What is the source of the circus' ongoing appeal and success, on every continent, from generation to generation? I believe it is the same appeal exerted by the *e*ternal *tarot* itself, and it is just this: *there is never only one thing going on*. And is it not true that many expressions of the political *arena* are derived from this context? A candidate "*throws his hat into the ring*", or "*goes for the brass ring*" of victory; demagogues "*play to the peanut gallery*", and lately there are allegations of an Elephant in the nation's living room![vi]

We shall see in due course that the history of the Republican Party, like that of the Tarot, is largely of a negative kind, and that, if the issue were to be accidentally cleared by the dissipation of puffery and flatulence, there is in fact no reliable history of ANYTHING before the 14th century of the Common Era! Deception and self-deception were in the mouths of the first political commentators and party flacks, and later analysts have done little more than reproduce this first false testimony, whether in good faith or bad, it matters not. As it so happens, all of the various commentators have worked within a narrow range, and owe, comparatively speaking, very little to inventive faculty. That is why no one else has had the idea of linking the Republican Party with these ancient, arcane symbols, and that is why *I* hope to "*make* a fortune" in helping credulous people to "*read*" them!

Regarding the symbols and nomenclature of the Republican Party, according to the online **Urban Dictionary**,[vii] a Republican is either, 1) "*An individual who believes that the white male Christian God should be the only object of worship on the planet, that power and wealth should remain in the hands of 1% of the world's population while the remaining 99% starve...*

and that America is the only real country on Earth while all... other countries ... are just fakes invented by communists...oh wait, it's terrorists now, isn't it?"; or, 2) "Someone who supports the rights of the unborn, but won't fund stem cell research that could help the millions who are already here. The first one to protest abortion rights, and the first... to take a life through capital punishment. Someone who espouses personal freedom, and then tries to pass constitutional amendments to restrict it. Someone threatened by government surplus but unfazed by government deficits. Someone who is pro-business but anti-citizen. Someone who wants to take away the helping hand, after he's made it to safety. Someone who holds a cross in one hand and tries to burn it with the other." If these judgments seem harsh, they have been voted most popular, from well over 130 proposed definitions, by thousands of visitors to this website, and thus, in the Electronic Republic, must surely be supposed the most correct? Lest these be thought only the recent opinions of an effete generation, one may ponder this old-timey expression from East Texas: "*A Republican can't enjoy his food unless somebody else is hungry.*"

The party is often called the "Grand Old Party", or G.O.P. Wags have noted that these initials may also stand for "Greedy On Purpose", "Gropy Ol' Pedophiles", etc. Such frivolity, of course, has no place in serious discussion; therefore, we shall not attempt to be serious!

The Elephant as symbol of the US Republican Party comes from an 1874 cartoon by Thomas Nast of *Harper's Weekly*, who also gave the Donkey to the Democratic Party. **Wikipedia** says that, when Alexander the Great's defeated the Indian king Porus, war elephants came to symbolize imperial power, e.g. on coins. White elephants (a religious symbol of Buddha), have often indicated royal power and prestige in Asia.[viii]

> "Elephants are... potentially dangerous..., capable of crushing and killing any other land animal, from rhinocerous and lions to humans. They can experience unexpected bouts of rage, and can be vindictive. In Africa... teenage elephants attack human villages in what is thought to be revenge for... massive cullings... In India, male elephants attack villages, destroy homes and kill people on a regular basis...
>
> "Adult male elephants... enter the periodic state called *musth* (Hindi for madness), sometimes spelt "must"... It is characterised by very excited

and/or aggressive behavior and a thick, tar-like liquid... discharge... through the temporal ducts from... glands on the sides of the head. Musth is linked to sexual arousal or establishing dominance, but this relationship is far from clear... [S]cientific investigation of musth is greatly hindered by the fact that even the most otherwise placid of elephants may actively try to kill any and all humans... [T]he tar-like secretion remains largely uncharacterised, due to the difficulties of collecting a sample for analysis."[ix]

Recently, as the unslakable thirst of US policymakers for oil at any cost has reached an unprecedented state of blind bloodymindedness, the conclusion has been reached by many observers that today's Republican leaders *musth* have oil on the brain, and yet I will posit with some confidence that none have reached this idea by a more circuitous route, seen through a glass more dark, than this! Then again, today's headlines continue to reveal a kind of sexual madness among some Republican officials, of which *mucth* remains to be said!

While looking through my own somewhat skewed rose-colored glasses, therefore, let me now introduce, with unheard-of wonder, marvels of arbitrary and groundless speculation as to the history of the Major Arcana, or, just how silly people can be. With reference to their form and number, it should scarcely be necessary to name them, for they must be almost commonly familiar if my venal venture is to succeed, but as it is precarious to assume anything, and as there are also other reasons, such as the need to pad out this work, I will tabulate them briefly as follows:

Some observers believe that Republicans are descended from dinosaur-like creatures; however, the opposite may also be true, according to the law of survival of the fittest..

Class I

§ 2

TRUMPS[x] MAJOR

Otherwise, Greater Arcana.

1. *The Magician,* the juggler, the dice-player, the vulgar trickster. Coyote, to Native Americans; Loki, to the Norse.

2. *The High Priestess,* the Secret Ingredient; ever new and improved.

3. *The Empress,* connected with the idea of universal nutti-and-fruitiness.

4. *The Emperor,* by imputation the grouse of the former.

5. *The Duffer,* called also the *Pope* or *Heirophant.* We agree with Waite that, in its primitive form, this card did *not* represent the Roman Pontiff. This is an example of "negative history".

6. *The Lovers,* also *Marriage.* This card has many variants, as may be expected from its subject. In some decks, it is "Civil Union"; in others, "D-I-V-O-R-C-E".

7. *The Chariot.* Seen in some decks drawn by two sphinxes, "it must not be supposed that such was its original form; the variation was invented to support a particular historical hypothesis."[xi] In the 18th century, white horses were shown yoked to the carriage. As regards the card's name, Waite tells us further that the Chariot is a King in the moment of triumph, "typifying... th(at) victory which creates kingship... and not... vested royalty..."[xii] Box office receipts create Hollywood royalty across the political spectrum.

8. *Justice.* I have reversed Waite's transfer of *Justice* from Card VIII to the eleventh position, and the resultant move of *Strength* from Card XI to the eighth spot, and placed them as Stuart Kaplan does in his many works, a more traditional choice. *Justice* is presumed to represent one of the four cardinal virtues in the Trumps Major;[xiii] as it happens, the fourth emblem is missing, rather like a certain 18-minute segment of tape missing from a certain President's secret White House recordings.[xiv] It has therefore become necessary for commentators to discover it at all

costs. They have done what was possible to do, and yet their research has not yet revealed the tarot's missing *Prudence*. Neither is it found in the halls of Congress.

9. *The Hermit.* A card of attainment rather than quest. It is said that the Hermit's lantern contains the Light of Occult Science and that his staff is a Magic Wand, but this is an enormous load of fabricated custard for the consumption and consolation of he who is not inaccurately called "the man in the street", of the same sort as "intelligent design", and "reality television".

10. *The Electoral Process.* Here is an invention in search of necessity! When only 70% of the eligible population registers to vote, how hard is it to steal an election? Also called the *Wheel of Fortune*, in keeping with our theme of three-ring mockery!

11. *Strength,* also called *Fortitude.* The ringmaster is usually shown closing the lion's mouth, rather than putting her head into it. In justification of the present picture, it is also said that the card represents the origin of all use of force; as in the phrase, "*She's just askin' for it!*" (If Iran, e.g., develops nuclear capacity; clearly, She invites attack). Again, this card is given the eighth position by Waite.

12. *Th- H-ng-d M-n.* In one shallow, yet plausible view, modern man bound by his necktie, mortgage, season tickets, electronic datebook, and other possessions. In more prevalent interpretations, he signifies sacrifice, yet such notions should be ascribed to the machinations of solve-or-spin doctors. The present modification was simply irresistible; its derivation obvious to childishly compulsive game-players.

13. *Death.* The presentation consistently embodies the bourgeois view of life, death, and transformation. In its current and patent meaning, especially a card of the death of Kings.[xv] This is *particularly* apt given our personification of *Death* as former President **Richard M. Nixon**, cousin to the exiled King of Albania.[xvi]

14. *Time,* or *Temperance.* I could not seem to grasp the concept of *Temperance,* as it seemed to have little relation to restraint, moderation, or forbearance. I am greatly indebted to P.D. Ouspensky's illuminating description[xvii] of Card XIV as the Angel of Time, and therefore named my *Trump XIV* in homage to Ouspensky's vision.

15. *The Devil.* In the 18th century, a symbol of animal cunning. Today, of mere human venality. Now beginning a 21st century, we may foresee Beelzebub as a virus; while it is almost certain that, to vanishing species across the globe, we are, ourselves, the Old Nick, and "global warming" but a foretaste of Hell.

16. *Watergate;* or, *The Tower.* Alternative titles include *Castle of Plutus* and *Tower of Babel.* In the latter, the falling figures are Nimrod and his ministers;[xviii] how similar to our own view! Unforeseen disaster is universally symbolized in late 20th century US political lore by the flubbed, Republican-engineered break-in at Democratic National Headquarters in 1972 -- "the Watergate Scandal." Witness the **Media**'s penchant, 40-odd years later, to name scandals by appending "-gate" to any word: "Debate-gate", "Travel-gate", "Japan-gate", "File-gate", "Contra-gate", and "Page-gate", are but a few, too tawdry to recount. Even the ubiquitous phone company, "Ma Bell",[xix] used the phrase "Rate Gate" in ads! "Propa*gate*", "conju*gate*", and "alle*gate*" are just *scandals waiting to happen*! It is already a crime in several jurisdictions to *congregate,* so watch your step, Citizen! "Water" is also a useful additive for assigning guilt by association; this alone should have kept then-Arkansas Governor **Bill** and Mrs. **Hillary Clinton** from touching "White*water*" stock with a 10-foot oar!

17. *The Star.* This card is taken by some as proof of the Delphinic origin of the Tarot. In this far-flung confabulation, space-faring dolphins from Sirius, the Dog Star, long ago visited Earth and brought cards to the Dogone people of Africa. The innocent and apparently hungry Dogone, prevented by impenetrable jungle canopy from ever having seen the sky, mistook the aliens for slave-traders, killed and ate them. Later study of various inedible objects brought by the devoured ambassadors as communications tools revealed to tribal elders much which had been hidden, leading them to regret their hasty actions. However, there was nothing to be done about it, and so they said, "*Doggone!*"

18. *The Moon.* In some versions, the moon is half-empty; in others; it is taken to be half-full. In our portrayal, it is more than half-assed.

19. *The Sun.* Behind the wall, Grandmother Spider of Native American mythology spins destinies. In another symbolical construct, a frightened peasant girl weaves gold from straw, and tries to guess the name of an evil dwarf. In our more pernicious view, a nervous government clerk is trapped in an elevator with an evil Senator; she doesn't have to guess his name or his game!

20. *The Supreme Court.* Vivacious dilettante Count de Gebelin, Waite's archaeologist/apotheosis, points out that, if only those *depressing* tombstones were removed, the card most often called *Judgment* could be seen as a symbol of creation.[xx] I have thus removed them, creating something even more depressing!

21. *The World*. An eloquent image of joy in the flesh, of intoxication in the earthly paradise, but guarded and guided by The Watchers. The rich prefer the Nanny State.

0. *The Fool*. In the age of electronic communications, some Internet iconoclasts identify this card with Steve Forbes, Bill Gates, Michael Dell; or even Hero-Nerd Mark Cuban. Waite for some vague reason places it twenty-first in his Sequence, while still numbering it zero (0), or null; he then places *The World* in twenty-second place, but numbers it *XXI*. This is so silly and arbitrary that even we can find no reason for continuing it! The "true" arrangement of the cards, of course, is anyone's guess, although it has been said to me that only by placing *The Fool* first in the sequence of Major Arcana is balance achieved among the four elements (air, fire, earth, water) associated with each card, as well as more nearly portraying the Seeker at the beginning of his or her Quest for Knowledge. Yet has it not been truly said that those who would fight City Hall are on a *Fool*'s errand, and will end as they began? Thus it may be with those who rely upon **The Republican Tarot**!

Class II

§ 3

THE FOUR SUITES
Otherwise, Lesser Arcana.

The resources of imitation having been squandered, if not profitably invested, in the twenty-two Trumps, the symbolism of which remains unquestionably vague, there remain four suits, which I have chosen to call "suites", echoing a more corporate feel, a more Euro-centric outlook, and, onomatopoetically, the kind of deal everyone wants. These suites, tarot's ancient Minor Arcana, which have become the Clubs, Diamonds, Hearts, and Spades of modern card games, are variously represented in many decks. Waite used Wands, Pentacles, Cups, and Swords. Kaplan's **Tarot of the Witches**[xxi] substitutes Batons for Wands/Clubs and Coins for Pentacles/Diamonds.

I follow Kaplan with *Coins*, cold cash being an ancient and timeless prerequisite for political success. *Coins* relate to material and financial matters. This is the suite of the merchant, the entrepreneur, the opportunist, and the adventurer. Associated with Earth, as in dirty work and mud-slinging. Wands/Batons/Clubs are *Bushes*, the suite of free enterprise and growth. They represent modest, humble persons. This is the suite of the logger and shrimper; of oil-field trash, underachieving students, failed businessmen and CIA spooks. Associated with the element of Fire, as in, "*After a forest fire, salvage what's left!*" Cups/Hearts have evolved -- or been intelligently designed? — into *Pineapples*,[xxii] a well-known symbol of love, gaiety, happiness, sexuality and fertility. Cards of this suite allude to deep feelings and passions, including those kept closeted. This is the suite of humane overseers and wise managers; however, in military parlance, a "pineapple" is a grenade. Associated with the element of Juice, as in, "*He has a lot of Juice on the Hill.*" Above all, the suite of the modern imperialist, the multi-national operator. Classic Swords/Spades have here a more modern image as *Arms*. *Arms* refer to force, strength, and authority, including moral or intellectual authority. They symbolize activity, for good or ill. This is the suite of civic leaders, lodge brothers, insurance salesmen, and career military families. *Arms* are linked with Air, as in, "*He blows a lot of hot air.*"[xxiii]

"Kings" in this deck are "Players"; while "Queens" are "Ladies". Since the United States has no royalty, the American President is officially "Mister President"; his wife. "First Lady".[xxiv] So far, no President has had powers comparable to those of a *real* hereditary monarch, although some have tried to appropriate them; and no First Lady has had powers comparable to those of, say, **Queen Elizabeth I** (**Mary Todd Lincoln** and **Eleanor Roosevelt** notwithstanding). But in the common, or "street", parlance, those who aspire to power at any level are called "players"; while their female companions, from the skankiest 'hos to the slickest harlots, are genteelly termed "ladies". I have merely elevated, or "lifted", these terms from the collective semi-consciousness.

The suite of Coins is led by two who defined rich Republicanism, former US Senator **Nelson Aldrich** (**R-RI**), and his socialite-philanthropist-asset daughter, **Abby Aldrich Rockefeller**, as Player and Lady. Bushes are led by former President **George H.W.** and First Lady **Barbara Bush**. Arms are marshaled by wartime Chairman of the Joint Chiefs of Staff and former Secretary of State, General **Colin Powell** (Ret.), and wartime Secretary of State **Condoleezza Rice**. The suite of Pineapples is personified by 1996 Presidential candidate, former US Senator (**R-KS**) and Majority Leader **Robert Dole** – *even though his family are not the pineapple Doles* – and his wife, former Labor Secretary, Transportation Secretary, and Director of the American Red Cross, **Elizabeth**.

From the beloved **Mother Goose** of a Euro-centric collective childhood, "Knights" are herein "Knaves", and these fellows *still* have a fondness for unauthorized tarts! Finally, the "Pages", or "Valets", of other *tarots* have here become "Varlets". A page, in American national and state congresses, is often a young, idealistic person who serves in order to learn; while the Varlets of **The Republican Tarot** are, rather, mostly ambitious scoundrels who serve themselves in order to profit! (In modern playing cards, Knaves and Varlets have become one fellow of questionable character, the "Jack". This may come from "jack-of-all trades", or, as in the current *patois* of the street, a "jacker", one who can both wheedle and needle, sell and tell, steal and deal, stack and mac; someone who is both fighter and back-biter, climber and two-timer.)

Finally, each suite contains ten numbered cards, each uniquely illustrated. The symbolism of these resides in their rank and in the suite to which they belong, so that even the smaller cards have a particular meaning attached to their number in connection with their particular suite. I reserve, therefore, the details of the Lesser Arcana, until I come to speak of them in the third part of this ridiculously redundant volume.

§ 4

THE TAROT IN HISTORY.

What is the tarot? What does the word *tarot* mean? Where and when did tarot originate? Is it really possible to see the future by examining Eternal meanings and transitory positions of tarot cards in the past and present? (Do you think I can *answer* these questions? You *are* a dreamer!) The origin of the word *tarot,* like the origin of the cards themselves, remains obscure despite a wealth of commentators, beginning with the ubiquitous Count de Gebelin in 1781, who spontaneously intuited,[xxv] upon learning of decks then extant in rural France, Italy, and on Sesame Street,[xxvi] that the word was Egyptian, referring to the "Road of Life", a reeking back alley in Old Cairo's Quarter of the De Nial.[xxvii] Later scholars and maniacs have variously attributed tarot and its symbols to lost utopian civilizations from Arcadia to Tibet; games played in Carthage and in Troy;[xxviii] and the designs you see behind your eyelids when you close 'em real tight.

Gypsies may have carried tarot cards from India westward in the 15th century; or Alexander's pack elephants[xxix] may have carried them across the Alps. Others trace the true tarot to secret Aramaic texts from before the time of Christ, or Beatles' lyrics played backwards from before the time of the Walrus. No one living today seems to really know, but anyone who is interested can find fascinating theories in many books, as well as in drug-induced altered states. The tarot readily takes on the symbolism of its times; thus, in Europe's Dark Ages, the cards were used to tell a forbidden story of Jesus of Nazareth's secret marriage to Mary Magdalene, their child, the early Church, and the Holy Grail.[xxx]

In modern times, the tarot has been popularized by dozens of schemers and charlatans, and decks based upon foundations as varied as women's spirituality, baseball, Native American lore, trolls, fairies both gay and straight, Arthurian legend, and Oriental philosophies; ethnicities from aborigine to other-worldly; authors as diverse as William Shakespeare, William Blake, and Jane Austen; and every "New Age" metaphysical fad from Angels to Zoroastrianism. But, *this is no New Age deck* – we are going back to the Dark Ages with the **Republican Tarot!**

§ 5

THE REPUBLICAN PARTY IN HISTORY.

For us, the pressing questions are: What are Republicans? Where and when did Republicans originate? Is it really possible to see into the future by examining transitory Republican positions and leaders of past and present? Like the tarot, the origins of the Republican Party are Veiled in Mystery; but in the latter case have been, I believe, *deliberately* obscured by *Jeffersonian Democracy!* Yes, that arch-radical of **Revolution**, that Frenchified, slave-holding hypocrite **Thomas Jefferson**, was the first US President elected by the *Republican* Party! In what seems, in hindsight, a successful liberal *coup d'état,* Jefferson and his Vice President, **Aaron Burr**, were chosen by an inexperienced, confused Congress, dominated by the *Federalist* Party, after each received an identical number of votes in the Electoral College! (After this trying experience, ballots for President and Vice President were counted separately – *duh,* **Founding Fathers**!)

In defining republicanism for future voters, Jefferson's party favored small government and states' rights. "Tricky Thomas" even advocated **Term Limits**, in a message to **Congress** in 1829: "*The duties of all public offices are... so plain and simple that men of intelligence may readily qualify themselves for their performance, and I can not but believe that more is lost by the long continuance of men in office than is... gained by their experience.*"[xxxi] On gun control, Jefferson is more patriot saint to the **Idaho Militia** than supporters of the **Brady Bill**: "*The strongest reason for the people to retain the right to keep and bear arms is, as a last resort, to protect themselves against tyranny in government.*" He further confused everyone by *keeping his promises* to friends and enemies alike! He abolished excise taxes and reduced the national debt. He also pioneered the bottom-line strategy of "*making all the banks Republican by sharing deposits among them in proportion to the disposition they show...*",[xxxii] a principle continuing, even as this work is composed, in controversial 2006 firings of Republican-appointed federal prosecutors deemed unreliable in their political thinking. Yet it must be said that, "To the victor goes the spoils", is a philosophy not limited to any particular ruling party, nor to any single nation or era.

Imagine the surprise of rank and file Republicans when Jefferson's party suddenly changed its name to *Democratic*! Such sneaky strategies threw *authentic* republicans – who, as Federalists, favored big government, school uniforms, and taxing codfish – into disarray for 60 years, when they rallied, employing free-wheeling dirty tricks themselves. The modern Republican Party was founded at Ripon, Wisconsin,[xxxiii] on the eve of the **Civil War**, by young scions of former Federalism. These "radical" Republicans wanted to *eradicate slavery* and *sow the South with salt*. Their moderate brethren (delicate womenfolk being excused from voting) only advocated stopping the *spread* of slavery, *limiting Black migration North*, and *lashing the South with wet noodles*. Together, they formed a majority party, which has endured to become modern Republicanism. This model, in which individuals from such disparate elements as the "Moral Majority" and actual Christians find common ground by not asking or telling plainly what they want, has typified the "G.O.P."[xxxiv] ever since! They call it the "Big Tent", covering disparate views; is it anyone's fault that the disparate views thus cozened and nourished are as misbegotten as the attractions of a sleazy freak show?

If party activists were confused, ordinary folks were baffled by political alignments of the pre-Civil War era. At the **Republican National Convention** of 1860, a plank favoring the **Declaration of Independence** was hissed off the floor, leaving a large, dangerous hole, then hammered back onto the platform by industrious anti-slavery delegates. The leading Republican newspaper in Missouri, the *Daily Missouri Democrat* (!?!?!), blared: "**White Men for Missouri and Missouri for White Men. Who's On First?**" This query survived in the national consciousness a century later in the comedy of **Bud Abbott** and **Lou Costello**.

The "new" Republican Party succeeded, as cartooning historian-philosopher **Larry Gonick** points out,

> "because [it] billed [itself] as the party of... [the] free, white, working man. Slavery... was wrong not only because of what it did to Blacks, but... what it did to the white worker. The 4 million slaves formed a low-paid labor pool, which competed with free workers. The slave system lowered wages, raised hours, eroded working conditions, and destroyed the... dignity of labor... This logic carried many Republicans... to... excluding even *free* Blacks from [new] territories. After all, 'everyone knew' that Blacks would work for lower wages than whites [*since white employers wouldn't pay them as much!*]"[xxxv]

The **Supreme Court**'s *Dred Scott* decision of 1857 (which, sadly, did *not* prohibit White suburban "mall rats" from wearing dreadlocks) gave credence to paranoid Northern Republicans, ruling that Congress couldn't restrict slavery, that Blacks had "no rights which the white man is bound to respect",xxxvi and that "*We are rubber; you are glue; it bounces off of us; we stick it to you*!" Would Northern Whites let themselves be enslaved? It was time to find out!

The first candidate of the born-again Republican Party, **John C. Fremont**, was defeated. **Abraham Lincoln**, the first lawyer President,xxxvii spread the party's "Big Tent" over both know-nothings (called "Know-Nothings") and out-and-out abolitionists (called "wild-eyed radicals"), winning a new majority. Democrats then split into Northern and Southern wings and self-destructed playing chicken (a favorite Democratic pastime ever since, along with pulling the "wishbone" and Uncle Bubba's finger). Lincoln, a wrestler,xxxviii let the South attack first, at Ft. Sumter, SC, a "provocation" carefully invited and swiftly repaid. The man we call **Great Emancipator** was in no hurry to *free* the slaves; he merely wished to prevent the *spread* of slavery to western settlements.

The **Emancipation Proclamation** of 1862 freed *only* slaves in rebel territory, where it was ignored. Only when Southern armies beat the North repeatedly did Lincoln turn to free Northern Blacks, and escaped slaves *begging* to kick some slave-o-crat butt, promising them that Union victory would end slavery throughout the US. A war of attrition led by hard-drinking General, and later Republican President **Ulysses S. Grant**, finally defeated the **Rebels**. Lincoln didn't live to enjoy his victory, becoming the first US President to die at the hands of an assassin and be re-born, like **Darth Vader**, at the hands of propagandists.

His program to bring the South back into the Union rapidly, allowing surviving slave-o-crats to resume control, died with him, while die-hard **Dixie** determination to keep the racist "old ways" was fanned by his death. **Black Codes**xxxix imposed virtual slavery on those whom fratricidal war had freed. Finally, the Republican-controlled Congress passed a program of **Radical Reconstruction** (over the veto of *Democratic* President Andrew **Johnson**, who, as Lincoln's Vice-President, had succeeded him – those "kinks" in the election process). Reconstruction included military occupation of Southern states, new state constitutions guaranteeing equal rights to Blacks, forced ratification of the 14th Amendment (the "equal protection" clause), and **Rhett** taunting **Scarlett**.

Thousands of Northern investors ("carpetbaggers") went South to take advantage of the new business climate,xl along with idealists, charlatans and grifters of every stripe. Black Southern legislatures voted for free public education, and Black voters sent Black Senators and Congressmen to Washington. The 15th Amendment, giving the vote to adult Black male citizens, ensured Grant's election in 1868. Some White Southerners turned to mob violence and hysteria; others to incest and moonshine. Some 40,000 former **Confederate** soldiers emigrated to **Brazil**; many thousands more moved **West**, or to **Mexico**. Until 1877, while the South was thus forcibly "reconstructed", and for a century after, White Republicans were rare as hens' teeth in **Dixie**.

A frenzy of economic growth and fortune-founding followed the **Civil War**. Gold was discovered in **California**. A transcontinental railroad was built, with gigantic public land giveaways to new railroad companies and free stock in them for cooperative elected officials all along the tracks. The Grant administration, the most corrupt in US history (until recently), set standards for graft and insider payoffs which still inspire imitators. Dumbed-down "Darwinism" justified genocide against **Native Americans** and the exploitation of **Black**, **Latin American**, and **Asian** workers,[xli] along with women and children, while "Manifest Destiny" beckoned with the rich resources of the American West.

The election of 1876 was close. Samuel "Tweedledee" **Tilden**, a "reform" Democrat,[xlii] ran against Rutherford B. "Tweedledum" **Hayes**, a "regular", pro-business Republican. Early returns favored Tilden, but Republicans challenged results in four states, accusing "the Democrats of intimidating Black voters with Ku Klux Klan tactics, while... Democrats charged... Republicans with buying votes. Both were correct."[xliii] A commission of eight Republican Congressmen and seven Democrats was appointed to settle the issue. It voted 8 to 7 for Hayes. Democrats were *so shocked*! To prevent another war of secession – and to get Union troops where they were *really* needed (out West, to "protect" railroad camps; and in new industrial cities, to crush the **General Strikes** of 1877 and later), a deal – the infamous **Hayes-Tilden Compromise** – was made to pull troops out of the South, where they had protected Blacks' rights since the Civil War. Reconstruction – and federal protection – ended overnight. A reign of terror put Blacks "in their place" – or their graves. Betrayed and abandoned, for a century afterward, Black Republicans were also rare in the South, as were Black voters of any persuasion!

Throughout the fabulous **Gilded Age**, until the end of the 1800s, "Republicans were distinguished from... Democrats chiefly by being successful."[xliv] Democrat "reformers" spent considerable righteous dismay on graft, corruption, and nasty practices in food handling, generally ignoring the plight of poor workers and farmers. The greatest prognosticator of his day, a German philosopher, lived, wrote, and died in abject poverty in England. His name was **Karl Marx**, and it may even be that *he* originated the tarot!

In the trumped-up **Spanish-American War**, which drove the failing **Spanish Empire** from the **Caribbean**, **Theodore Roosevelt** led a staged cavalry charge (observed by embedded reporters) up **San Juan Hill** on the island of **Puerto Rico**. "T.R."'s stated foreign policy, "*Speak softly and carry a big stick*", is still favored in many quarters. His "progressive Republicanism" promoted anti-trust laws. Born to wealth and privilege, "Teddy" was a rancher, trophy hunter, police commissioner and an intended victim of assassination during his long, lively career. He became President upon the assassination of **William McKinley** in 1901. He popularized the novel concept of *conserving national resources*, so that they might be exploited later. He was the first President to jog in public; however, he did *not* wear jogging shorts.[xlv] The "Teddy bear" was named for him. Roosevelt refused re-nomination after two terms in the **Oval Office**,[xlvi] and sailed to **Africa** to hunt big game. Four years later, he tried to regain office, but was defeated for the Republican nomination by **William Taft**, his successor. T.R. became the candidate of the wild and woolly **Progressive** ("Bull Moose") Party in 1912. He didn't win, but split the Republican vote, and a Democrat was elected.

From 1920 -- 1933 the US participated in a reforming social experiment, **Alcohol Prohibition**. For 13 years, production, sale, and use of intoxicating beverages, from beer to brandy, were legally forbidden everywhere nationwide. To readers who may find interest in comparing that experience with our own era's so-called "**War on Drugs**", I highly recommend Mr. Thomas M. Coffey's excellent history of the time, which I here quote briefly, from the Foreword, as he recalls the social influences which led to the "noble experiment":

> ... the puritan ethic of the people who founded the country and of their descendants; the[ir] unswerving belief... in the virtues of hard work, piety, and sobriety; their religious fundamentalism and uneasiness about intellectual freedom; their fear of the immigrants huddled in the cities and the religions (Catholicism and Judaism)... "foreigners" had brought with them; the conviction, especially among employers, that alcohol diminished the productivity of workers; the growing certainty on the farms and in the small towns that city life encouraged alcoholic (and therefore sexual) excess – a certainty fostered by the sordidness of the old-time saloons and brothels, and by the well-advertised drinking habits of the urban poor.[xlvii]

And, regarding certain similarities between that time and this:

> The parallels between our current narcotics prohibition and the alcohol prohibition of the 1920s are too striking to ignore. No one can deny the need for some kind of program to counteract the personal and social tragedies which arise out of alcohol and drug abuse. It is appallingly

ironic; however, that the same methods which totally failed to suppress alcohol, which on the contrary stimulated its greater use, should now be employed against narcotics. No one ought to be surprised that this latter-day prohibition is as ineffectual, and indeed as aggravating to the problem, as the older one. All the means of circumvention and subversion developed [then] are in widespread practice today. The smuggling, hijacking, bribery, corruption, political maneuvering, gang warfare, and disrespect for law which became institutions in America during the '20s operate again in the '70s .[xlviii]

As a **Constitutional amendment**, Prohibition was a bipartisan folly, the excesses of which cannot be laid at the door of any one party. Passed during the Democratic administration of **Woodrow Wilson**, it was enforced by Republicans **Warren G. Harding**[xlix], **Calvin Coolidge**[l], and **Herbert Hoover**[li], and its end came only with the election of Democrat **Franklin D. Roosevelt**, although with support from many thirsty Republicans, and to the dismay of moralists of both parties. Indeed, influential **Republican Women**, finally outraged by the lawlessness and hypocrisy of Prohibition, made it possible for it to be repealed.

Five Democratic administrations, including Roosevelt's "New Deal", **World War II**, and the detonation of the atom bomb passed before Republicans came to power again, with the 1952 election of victorious retired General and grandfather-figure **Dwight D. ("Ike") Eisenhower**. It is from the Eisenhower era to date, and from recent headlines wherever fancy struck, that many incidents and characters have been drawn for the **Republican Tarot**; however, it is vital to realize that qualified Republican candidates for *each* and *every* card might have been culled from *any* era, or party, of our nation's yet-brief history. That fact, it is devoutly to be hoped, will make the archetypes herein recognizable to many among the still-breathing-and-consuming, despite the short-term memory loss which our information century so encourages with an ever-changing cast of appalling, and thus newsworthy, celebrities. Most of my post-1950s fictions are more fully elucidated in a following section; while many of the pre-Eisenhower figures which adorn the cards have been highlighted and described more fully in the present one. In this way, the Seeker must flip back and forth in the book, time after time, searching for correlations in several different sections, phrases vaguely recalled and chapters cunningly titled, with all most confusingly arranged! This will lead to many additional book sales, when the paper wears out with constant handling![lii]

PART II
The Doctrine Behind the Veil

§ I
THE REPUBLICAN PARTY AND SECRET TRADITION

Former Presidents **Thomas Jefferson** and **John Quincy Adams** both died on July 4th, 1826, 50th anniversary of the signing of the **Declaration of Independence**. **Calvin Coolidge** was born July 4th, 1923.[liii]

James A. Garfield (1831-1881), 20th President of the United States, was the first ambidextrous President.[liv] He needed to use both hands, as he remains the only man to have simultaneously served in Congress (**R-OH**), as Senator-elect, and as President-elect, and the only Congressman sent directly to the Presidency. While in Congress, on taxpayers' time, Garfield discovered a novel proof of the Pythagorean Theorem. He was assassinated,[lv] and his name appropriated by a complacent cartoon cat.

Garfield's Vice-President and successor, **Chester A. Arthur** (1829-1886, 21st President), inaugurated the Electric Age when he pushed a button at the **White House** that set machinery in motion at a **New Orleans** exposition.[lvi] Before his election, Arthur worked at the **Port of New York** for the **Grant** administration, and was fired by Grant's successor, President **Hayes** (he of the **Compromise**), under suspicion of bribery and corruption. As President, Arthur's agenda included establishing the **Civil Service**, or "entrenched bureaucracy", winning him the title, "Father of the Mother of All Red Tape".[lvii] A fashionable man, he insisted on the redecoration of the White House before moving in, and had 24 wagonloads of furnishings carried out and sold at public auction.[lviii]

Benjamin Harrison (1833-1901), 23rd President, was a grandson of **William Henry Harrison**, "Old Tippecanoe", the 9th.[lix] The only President from **Indiana**, Harrison, a one-term wonder, crafted the first billion dollar budget, an early use of **New Math**.[lx]

William McKinley, 25th Chief Executive, was shot and killed in 1901 at the **Pan-American Exposition** in **Buffalo, NY** by anarchist **Leon Czolgosz**. Czolgosz was electrocuted two months later at **Auburn State Prison**,[lxi] again heralding the Electrical Age.

William H. Taft (1857-1930), 27th President, was also the 10th **Chief Justice** of the **Supreme Court**, so far the only person to have held both of these positions; however, *he did not hold them at the same time*, as has seemed the goal of some of his successors.[lxii] Taft, a slender young man, eventually weighed over 300 pounds, pioneering American obesity.[lxiii]

Theodore Roosevelt wrote over 40 books on history, politics, and adventure. While inspecting construction of the **Panama Canal**, he became the first President to leave US soil while in office. He was the first to ride in an automobile, fly in an airplane, and go down in a submarine; it is not known who went down with him.[lxiv]

Herbert Hoover (1874-1964), first President born west of the **Mississippi River**, developed a rich gold mine in **Australia** while in his 20s, and was a multimillionaire in his 30s. A few days after he was sworn in as 31st President, the **Stock Market** abruptly crashed, ushering in the **Great Depression**[lxv] and jump-starting **American folksinging**.

Strom Thurmond (1901-2003), so far the only US Senator elected by a write-in vote, as a **South Carolina** Democrat in 1954,[lxvi] ran for President (1948) on the racist **States Rights Democratic** ("Dixiecrat") ticket, and became a Republican in 1964. He was re-elected to the Senate, where he served until 2003, resigning at age 100. Thurmond, a "kingmaker" for **Richard Nixon** in 1968, held the South against **Ronald Reagan** at the **Republican National Convention**, and fended off Alabama Governor **George Wallace**'s third-party candidacy by being more-racist-than-thou. Notoriously fond of young women, he tried to date one of **Lyndon Johnson**'s high-school age daughters when he was nearly 60; LBJ just said, "*No!*" One Senator said of Strom, "When he dies they'll have to beat his pecker down with a baseball bat... to close the coffin lid."[lxvii]

Between retiring from the **Army** and winning the Presidential election of 1952, "**Ike**" **Eisenhower** served as President of **Columbia University**.[lxviii] When angry students briefly seized the University President's office there years later, in 1968, they found Eisenhower's "little black book" in a dusty file cabinet, containing names and phone numbers of dozens of attractive young **Defense Corporations**.

In case you have not had e-mail for the last ten years, **Abraham Lincoln** went to Congress in 1847. **John F. Kennedy** went to Congress in 1947. Lincoln became President in 1861; Kennedy, in 1961. Both men were deeply involved with civil rights. Both had wives who lost children while in the White House. Both were shot on Friday, in the head. **John Wilkes Booth**, who killed Lincoln, was born in 1839. **Lee Harvey**

Oswald, who in the official version of Kennedy's death was a "lone assassin", was born in 1939. Both killers were known by three names, in each case totaling 15 letters. Lincoln was shot in a theater called "Ford"; Kennedy in a car called "Lincoln", made by "Ford". Lincoln was shot in a theater; his assassin hid in a warehouse. Kennedy was shot *from* a warehouse; his assassin hid in a theater. Both Booth and Oswald were killed before being tried. Both Lincoln and Kennedy were succeeded by men named **Johnson**. A week before Lincoln was shot, he was in **Monroe, Maryland**. A week before Kennedy was shot, he was in **Marilyn Monroe**!

Both **George H.W. Bush** and **Richard Nixon** were in **Dallas**, on completely unrelated matters and without crossing paths, on the day **Kennedy** was killed there. Democratic Texas Governor **John Connally**, then-Vice President **Lyndon Johnson's** *protegé*, wounded in the attack, later was Nixon's Treasury Secretary and, when LBJ died, a Republican.

Richard Nixon, the first US President to receive a $200,000 annual salary, remains the only person twice elected Vice President and twice President.[lxix] **Gerald Ford**, born Leslie King. Jr.,[lxx] is the only person to be Vice President and President before ever running for either office.[lxxi]

From 1948 -- 1962, **George H.W. Bush** was a "simple oil man". In 1975, whent President **Ford** tired of his nagging, Bush became Director of the **Central Intelligence Agency**. In 1989, by-then-President **Bush** sent US troops into **Panama** to overthrow Dictator-General **Manuel Noriega**. Noriega was brought to trial for drug trafficking.[lxxii] However, it emerged that his trading partner, for many years, had been the CIA!

Official records about President **George W. Bush**, second son of **G.H.W.** and **Barbara Bush**, and his family have an odd way of disappearing. There is little evidence, other than rumor, that he ever attended **The University of Texas at Austin**, but tales are told.[lxxiii] Bush's driving and arrest records are reportedly incomplete. Joining a **Texas Air National Guard** unit, rather than going to **Vietnam**, where there was a war on at the time, he missed drills and inspections, was suspended from flying and sent home early, but still got paid, and saw no active duty. First Lady **Laura Bush** had a car wreck as a teenager in which her then-boyfriend died. No charges were filed. (Her family owns half of **Odessa**, y'all.) George and brother **Jeb**'s children have all had legal problems, and perhaps drug and/or drinking issues, but these have been dealt with "quietly", and with few consequences. Kid brother **Neil** cost taxpayers millions in a loan industry melt-down, but later sold educational software to school districts nationwide – hopefully *not* teaching kids how to manage their money! It is pointed out by cynics that *Dubya's Daddy ran the C.I.A.*

Campaign buttons boosting past Republican candidacies.

§ 2
THE TRUMPS MAJOR AND THEIR INNER SYMBOLISM

I
The Magician

One of the most admirable-seeming figures of the **Tarot**, idol of the radical right of the 1990s, radio talk show innovator **Rush Limbaugh** is *The Magician*, beaming with confidence and self-assurance. Above his head floats the mysterious medium of the public airwaves, an invisible cord here rendered visible, the *only* sign of life acknowledged by many devotees. He wears a stately robe, and displays on a table before him symbols of the four **Republican Tarot** suites (a *Pineapple*, a *Coin*, an AK-47 for *Arms*, and a small *Bush*), signifying the elements of unnatural, or political life, which he adapts as he wishes through the Magick of Technology. He grasps the Magick Limbaugh Stick, while in homes across the nation a growing chorus mutters, "How *low* can he *go?*"

Under the table, so to speak, or on an unconscious plane, telephones represent Mankind's aspirations to be in accord with the adept; a dumb, cynical hope that things can somehow be "wired". Suggested throughout is a gift for communication, but the power is limited to the gifted: the *Magician* is *most* impressive when his mouth is quicker than your mind!

This is the card for Aries, birth-sign of pyromaniacs and others who play with fire. The *Magician*'s fate recalls the story of Icarus, who flew too near the *Sun* and fell to Earth. What goes up must come down, even audience share! The first nationally syndicated radio pundit in 1988, Limbaugh was instrumental in Republicans' 1994 Congressional victory, having expanded his influence to cable television in 1992. His campaign against "drugs" ("*Drug use destroys societies.*") wore thin when it was learned that Limbaugh was addicted to prescription pain pills. As with many celebrities, a stint of "rehabilitation" (See *Trump II, The High Priestess*) relieved him of criminal consequences, proof positive of his Magickal powers!

I

The Magician

II
The High Priestess

Former First Lady **Betty Ford** is the *High Priestess* in our deck, Woman in Her Aspect as Co-Dependent. The scroll in her hands is inscribed with the word *Recovery*. It is partly covered with her mantle, inferring that some things are spoken and some things are implied. The visible portion recalls the old conundrum, "*The statement on the other side is true*" written on one side of a scroll, and "*The statement on the other side is false*" written on the opposite side. An exposed scar recalls Mrs. Ford's courageous battles against breast cancer, arthritis, addictions to booze and painkillers, and marriage to the clumsiest President in US history. She is seated between the black and white pillars – B and F – of the Betty Ford Institute, and the embroidered Veil of the Institute is behind her; behind it, much remains hidden by privilege. She symbolizes the inner light and truth which comes to the wise one who studies Criminal Law and discovers the Loophole of Rehabilitation.

There is another, deeper, more profound symbolism within this card, one which speaks to innermost desire, but it must not be spelled out!

The High Priestess

III
The Empress

Former First Lady **Nancy Reagan** is a stately figure, seated, wearing rich clothing, and with a holier-than-thou aspect. She sits in a field of artificial-looking flowers, before a darkening wood. As ever, she seems totally oblivious to her surroundings. In one interpretation, she is blocking the observer's view into the darkening mind of her husband, former President and Alzheimer's patient **Ronald**. While the *Empress* traditionally upholds family values above all, her own children are nowhere to be seen.

Both Mr. and Mrs. Reagan were influential Hollywood actors (her stage name was Nancy Davis) during the heyday of the House UnAmerican Activities Committee's (HUAC) Communist witchhunts; neither was ever blacklisted.

Nancy Reagan had a personal astrologer before she and "Ronnie" came to the White House and for a time afterward, until rude publicity caused her to put her psychic friend aside. However, after an unsuccessful assassination attempt on her husband, she returned to consulting the *Stars*, the **Media** be damned!

III

The Empress

IV
The Emperor

The *Emperor* is seen as former President **Ronald Reagan** (*left*, 1911-2004) enthroned on the Big Screen, ever his favored venue. Given his dress, youthful appearance, and co-star, film scholars place this scene as being from *Bonzo Goes to Washington*.

Note that while the *Sun* shines brightly on-screen, there is a night sky beyond. This alludes to Reagan's notoriously sunny outlook on problems (homelessness, joblessness, international ridicule) endured by ordinary Americans. The Snack Bar in front of the movie screen symbolizes the disinformation, diversions and cheap substitutes for value Reagan used to great effect to distract the gullible from substantive solutions. In a snack-related example, Reagan rebutted charges of declining quality in federally-supported school lunches by declaring ketchup a vegetable.

Reagan's movie hero roles often seemed to confuse – or amuse – him in real life. While Governor of California (1967-75), during demonstrations at San Francisco State College, he expressed his willingness to "*Let the bloodbath begin*". In 1969, during pro-People's Park demonstrations at UC Berkeley, he sent California Highway Patrol officers to quell students. Protests increased, and officers shot and killed a 25-year-old man and injured others. As 40th President (1981-89), he once did a "mic check" by intoning, "*We begin bombing in three minutes.*" Castigating the Soviet Union as an "Evil Empire" and favoring development of a space-based "Death Star" to combat it, he nevertheless held discussions with then-Soviet Premier Mikhail Gorbachev which ended the Cold War between the two superpowers. However, he also ordered an invasion of the small island nation of Grenada in 1983, when a self-identified "Marxist" slate was democratically elected there.

When faced with a question to which he didn't know the answer, or the answer to which was inconvenient, Reagan often resorted to outright, bald-faced lies. Known as the "Teflon President" because none of his fabrications ever damaged him politically, it is for this ability to remain wildly popular regardless of his policies' results that his years in office are ensconced in the Republican pantheon as the "Reagan Era."

IV

The Emperor

Reagan remains the only person elected US President who had been divorced; from actress Jane Wyman, said to have scoffed at his political ambitions. Marrying another actress, **Nancy** Davis, "Ronnie", then a "New Deal Democrat" – he went Republican in 1962 – became President of the Screen Actors' Guild (SAG). While his public testimony before the House Un-American Affairs Committee (HUAC, 1947-52) was typically vague and sanctimonious, both he and Nancy named Hollywood "Reds" to the Feds. It is mildly interesting that **Richard Nixon** was on HUAC while in Congress ('47-50). He is best known in that regard for the infamous Alger Hiss case, but HUAC's Hollywood investigations, including the **Reagans'** stool pigeoning, also took place during that time. No love was ever lost between the two ambitious California Republicans!

The most morally bankrupt policies of the Reagan Era were perhaps those of the **Iran-Contra**[lxxiv] "incident", when the US brokered illegal arms trades between two nations it sought to destabilize, Iran and Nicaragua, as well as cocaine exports by Nicaraguan "Contras" to the US. Part of the Iranian deal involved trading arms for hostages. The 1980 presidential campaign had taken place in the shadow of the "Iran hostage crisis", with **Media** networks reporting frequently on President Jimmy Carter's failure to free US hostages while Reagan fumed theatrically in the wings. He won the vote. "[A]llegations have been made...concerning a purported deal between high-level Reagan... operatives ... and... the Iranian government.... Although [Congressional] investigations in the 1990s declared [it]... unfounded, the conspiracy... remains a subject of... conjecture. [Its] exact nature... lies in a potential violation of the International Commerce Acts of 1798, which prohibit any private citizen or party from negotiating with a foreign power in matters of national policy or military action. It is alleged by... opponents that the Reagan campaign... communicated with the Iranian[s]... and asked them to extend the hostage crisis long enough to ensure that he won... The main cause for suspicion was the seeming coincidence of... the hostages' release *six minutes after Reagan was sworn into office* [in] 1981, as well as [his] later decision to provide arms to the anti-U.S. Iranian government, allegedly in return not for freeing the hostages, but for delaying their release". (*Italics added*)[lxxv] During the Itan-Contra revelations of 1986, it was little wonder that conspiracy theorists had so much fun with the earlier hostage crisis, sometimes called "The October Surprise".

V
The Duffer

The *Duffer*, or Bagman, is seen here in the guise of former Vice-President and President **Gerald Ford** (1913-2006), best remembered for his hasty pardon of his predecessor, the Burglar-President, **Richard Nixon**. At the time of his death, Ford was the longest-lived President, 93; lending credence to the old saw, "Only the good die young." He is (at time of writing) the only post-World War II President *not* to have considered alerting US nuclear forces.

Ford was the first person appointed Vice President under the 25th Amendment, in 1973. Before ascending to that lofty post, he was an Eagle Scout and played football for the University of Michigan, where he led his team to two undefeated seasons. As a senior, Ford became the only future US President to tackle a future Heisman Trophy winner, running back Jay Berwanger, who would win the first Heisman the following year. Ford then became a member of the US House of Representatives (**R-MI**), where he served for 24 years; as Minority Leader for eight. He wrote no major legislation, but President Lyndon Johnson appointed him to the Warren Commission, investigating the death of Johnson's predecessor, John Kennedy. In 1997, the Assassination Records Review Board (ARRB) said that Ford had altered the Warren Commission report, years earlier, to support the Magick single bullet theory. Despite this service, Johnson reportedly said of Ford at the time, "*He can't fart and chew gum at the same time.*"

Minority Leader Ford was appointed Vice-President when **Nixon**'s first Veep, Spiro Agnew, pled 'no contest' to money-laundering and tax evasion. When Nixon himself resigned over the *Watergate* affair, Ford became the 38th President. He told voters he was "a Ford, not a Lincoln". Few disagreed. Ford appointed former New York Governor Nelson **Rockefeller** as his Vice President and **George H. W. Bush** as liaison to the People's Republic of China, later Director of the CIA. His first Chief of Staff was former Congressman (**R-IL**) and Ambassador Donald Rumsfeld. In 1975, Rumsfeld became the youngest-ever Secretary of Defense. A young Wyoming politician, **Richard Cheney**, then became Chief of Staff, later managing Ford's 1976 Presidential bid.

V

The Duffer

Ronald Reagan launched his first Presidential run in 1975, winning several primaries. Conservatives convinced Ford to drop **Rockefeller** as Veep in favor of Senate Majority Leader **Bob Dole (R-KS)**. Ford won the nomination; but Democrat Jimmy Carter won the general election. After winning the Republican nomination in 1980, Reagan considered Ford as a running mate. But negotiations broke down when Ford offered instead to be "co-President", controlling key appointments (e.g., **Henry Kissinger** as Secretary of State, Alan Greenspan at Treasury). Reagan gave the Vice-Presidency instead to **George H. W. Bush**.

In 2001, Ford told *Detroit News* columnist Deb Price that there should be laws against anti-**Gay** discrimination, and hoped that Republicans would reach out to these voters. In an interview with Bob Woodward of *The Washington Post*, released after his death, Ford disagreed "very strongly" with **George W. Bush**'s use of alleged weapons of mass destruction to justify invading **Iraq**, calling it a "big mistake"[lxxvi]

The *Duffer* is seated between two pillars, but they are not the same pillars which the *High Priestess* guards; rather, they resemble golf bags, and his seat a tee. In his left hand is a scepter topped by a dollar sign; with his left he makes the well-known ecclesiastical sign of the encircled forefinger and thumb, signifying that the fix is in. A set of keys lies crossed before him. The Duffer holds the power of the keys; that is, he is the channel of institutional grace, as opposed to that of Nature, generally a law-abiding entity. An "M" on his sweater signifies that he is a Michigan *Wolverine*.

The *Duffer* is also the card of Libra, the indecisive, easily-swayed weathercock of astrological birth signs.

VI
The Lovers

David and **Julie Nixon Eisenhower** are The *Lovers* of the **Republican Tarot**. Heedless of the armed agents ("The Watchers") who have been their companions since childhood, the grandson of former President **Eisenhower** and the eldest daughter of his Vice President (later President), **Nixon**, walk hand-in-hand at twilight beneath a lovers' moon. Their wedding was the first outdoor nuptials celebrated at the White House.[lxxvii] They have eyes only for each other. Symbolic of Adam and Eve before the Fall, this card is also associated with the passionate, ill-tempered, egotistical, self-serving, blame-gamer's sign of Scorpio, itself associated with Pluto.[lxxviii]

VI

The Lovers

VII
The Chariot

This is the card of Sagittarius, the Zodiac's Archer, who makes strong men quiver, and women loose their buttons and bows. The card is also associated with Mars, God of War. Our *Chariot* is unusual only in that it is drawn, or pulled, by a rabbit and a zebra. The *Chariot*eer is seen as National Rifle Association President and spokesman, Republican activist, and Hollywood legend **Charlton Heston** (1924 -).

"Chuck" Heston has appeared on film as Judah Ben Hur, Moses, at least three US Presidents, and as the hope of humanity in *Planet of the Apes*. And it has gone to his head.

Heston's "Arena PAC" (Political Action Committee) makes financial contributions to candidates, but its main stock-in-trade is *Heston himself*, whose appearance at a campaign fundraising event could guarantee its success. Heston, unlike fellow thespians, former California Governor **Ronald Reagan** and present Governor Arnold Schwarzenegger, did not throw his hat, only his money and his fame, into the arena on the wild side of the silver screen.

VII

The Chariot

VIII
Justice

Here is Virgo, *e*ternal virgin of the Zodiac, poster-child of abstinence. Yet it is not by physical purity, but by firm obtuseness and lack of snap -- a sort of perpetual mental virginity -- that Virgoans are fondly known.

Justice is "in some ways, a sinister card... She administers the last test to the developing soul, who, upon successfully meeting her, emerges from the inner temple as [*Th_ H_ng_d M_n.*] In her positive aspect, *Justice* represents Reality and Truth, no matter how awe-full or horrifying they may seem to be. Reversed, she signifies that Prophetess whose auguries are vociferously denied, as were those of Cassandra."[lxxix] She appears here as **Martha Mitchell,** wife of **Richard Nixon**'s Attorney General, John. Her unfortunate gift of gab made her *persona non grata* among G.O.P. partisans during the *Watergate* debacle. Known as the "Mouth of the Potomac", Mrs. Mitchell "began contacting reporters when her husband's role in the scandal became known. At one time, Martha insisted she was held against her will in a California hotel room and sedated to keep her from making phone calls to the **Media**. She was discredited and... abandoned by most of her family... Nixon aides even leaked to the press that she had a 'drinking problem'. The Martha Mitchell effect, in which a psychiatrist mistakenly diagnoses [an] extraordinary but reasonable belief as a delusion, was later named after her. **Nixon** told... David Frost (in... 1977 on *Frost On America*), 'If it hadn't been for Martha Mitchell, there'd have been no Watergate.'"[lxxx]

Portrayed, as are others among the most ancient and mysterious tarot symbols, as standing between two pillars, Mrs. Mitchell appears to have just hung some dirty laundry on the White House *porte cochere*.

John Mitchell, by the way, testified that, although he was head of the Committee to Re-elect the President, chief law enforcement officer of the nation, and Nixon's former law partner, never once did the President ask him what he knew about Watergate.[lxxxi] Sentenced to 2 ½ -- 8 years in prison for his role in the break-in and cover-up, the sentence was later reduced, and he served only 19 months before being released for medical reasons.[lxxxii] Still, this demonstrates incontrovertibly, along with his marriage to Martha, that *Justice* does prevail!

VIII

Justice

IX
The Hermit

Abraham Lincoln, our *Hermit*, is at once the best-known, best-beloved, least understood and most misrepresented of all Republican Presidents. While the words "simple backwoods lawyer" follow his name as the words "poop in the woods" follow a bear, Lincoln was a successful railroad lawyer and a sophisticated philosopher. He maintained a distinguised correspondence, and, if any extraterrestrials were around during his lifetime, he was quite probably in touch with them.[lxxxiii] A man of warmth and good humor, he was quite odd in appearance,[lxxxiv] enduring ridicule, as well as personal tragedy, without whining. The first Republican President of the "modern era", Lincoln was also the first US President to die at the hands of a "lone nut" and be re-born at the hands of propagandists.

His public life and career were dominated by the issue of slavery, as he led the North to victory over the secessionist, slave-holding South in the US Civil War; and it is as "The Great Emancipator" that he is best remembered. In truth, Lincoln cared not a fig for freeing the slaves, but would have done anything possible and necessary to preserve the Union. Abraham Lincoln received his death wound while at a play, leading one to reflect upon the tragic, Shakespearean quality of his life. A century later, another war President, Lyndon B. Johnson, was parodied, off-Broadway, in a play called *MacBird!*[lxxxv] An equivalent effort for Lincoln might be called *AbraHamlet!* (*"To free or not to free? That is the question..."*)

On this card, the *Hermit* holds a lantern aloft while standing on an eminence. While the imagery reminds some of the tale of Diogenes, this Hermit is not looking for an honest man. Waite says that a *Star* is inside the lantern; if so, it is a fallen star indeed. In the valley below, a river runs with blood. Soldiers in blue and grey uniforms litter its banks. The **Banks**, however, are doing quite well.

The card is associated with Capricorn, the saturnine, surly goat of the Zodiac. Let us also not forget the scapegoat, who periodically carries the sins of the people into the wilderness and is devoured by them.

IX

The Hermit

X
The Electoral Process

In this card of great antiquity, the *Electoral Process*, surrounded by creatures of the coming Apocalypse (in the angles: Police of the Police State, the Ostrich of Isolationism, the Dried Bones of Entrenched Interests, and the predatory Cat of *Laissez-faire* Attitudes; these presided over by the Great Grouch ["*Cut the funds for Sesame Street!! What do I care?*"]), and supported from below by *Nextyme*, the Lizard of Eternal Chance, dominates the picture, also known as the *Wheel of Fortune*. In the center of the Wheel, we may catch a glimpse behind the Veil of the voting booth – is that a rolling "ball" (or *ball*ot) or a winking eye? – and, some may even see the Fickle Finger of Fate!

This is the ultimate game for political activists of every stripe. In the end it all comes down to the spin of the wheel, the roll of the dice, the luck of the draw; how one candidate looks shifty on television, and another grabs the brass knuckles and buys the voting machine factory.

X

The Electoral Process

XI
Strength

Also known as *The Force*, *Strength* is a card of varying interpretations. Here, **Angry White Males** are represented by a lion in a circus ring, who is being tempted by a buxom maiden, or "femi-Nazi"[lxxxvi], to bite her head off. The maiden is thought to represent **Political Correctness**; in some readings, she may be seen as **Diversity** herself. The lion seems dubious of the proffered morsel. The crowd watches hopefully.

"Angry white men" flocked to the Republican Party as the 20th century waned, becoming its *Strength*, disgruntled with perceived injustices of affirmative action and stoked by right-wing spin doctors. Incidents such as the 1995 Oklahoma City Federal Building bombing make us ask if this lion has enough "inner strength" to resist widely administering the Law of the Jungle! This is, obviously enough, the card for Leo, the astrological Lion, known for having expensive, pointless hobbies; shallow values; and little patience.

The growth of Diversity in the passing years has made some white men even angrier; others, more dubious of past totemic beliefs. Immigration issues may be discussed over a bowl of Vietnamese phō noodles or at the acupuncturist's ("*Asian kids study so hard they win all the scholarships!*" on the one hand; "*Acupuncture helped me when my doctor said, 'Get used to the pain or take morphine'!*" on the other).

On another level, the card may reference the Old Testament story of the Prophet Daniel in the den of lions, who was not eaten. *Why not?* Were the lions too well fed? Were they distracted by catnip, or by straw gladiators? Was Daniel's odor unsavoury?

XI

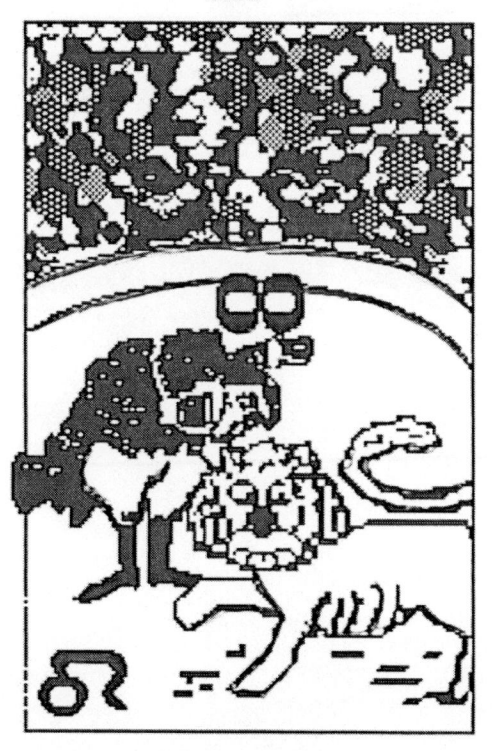

Strength

XII
Th_ H_ng_d M_n

John Q. Public, the Average Guy, Taxpayer, Regular Joe, Idiot, is *Th_ H_ng_d M_n*. Note that his foot is held but loosely in the triangular noose atop the civic gallows: there is an element of choice -- or, in some readings, *lack of initiative* -- in his quandary. The gallows from which he is suspended forms a *Tau* cross, while *Th_ H_ng_d M_n*'s legs form a fylfot cross, whatever the heck that is! There is a halo of questions about the head of the seeming martyr. Observe his trance-like expression; this is the highest product of Western Civilization! To understand the paradox of *Th_ H_ng_d M_n*, one must enter the Voteless Voting Booth.

Either the figure's hands are held behind him, or the game is not yet over. Are his hands tied? Is he holding anything? Has he anything up his sleeve? *We do not know.* Waite says, "We may exhaust all published interpretations and find only vanity."

XII

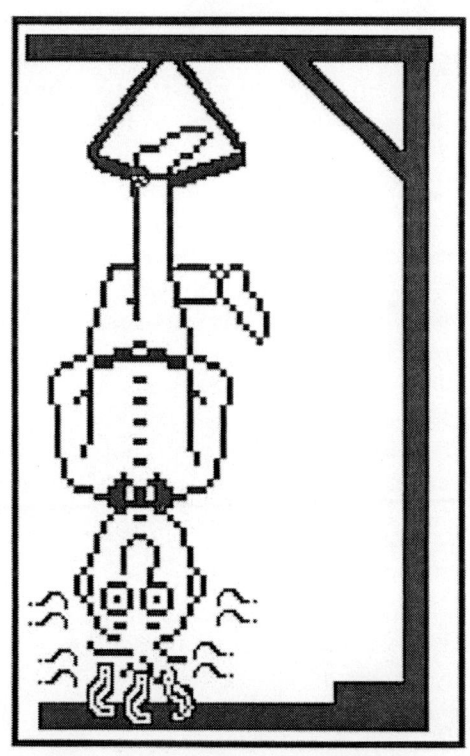

Th_ H_ng_d M_n

XIII
Death

No figure in the history of the Republican Party is more fitted to serve as our symbol of endings and beginnings than 36th President **Richard M. Nixon** (1913-1994). He got his start in used tires as a Washington rubber-rationing bureaucrat in World War II. Elected to Congress (**R-CA**), in a vicious, mud-slinging race, Nixon came to national notice as a lackey of red-baiting Senator **Joseph McCarthy (R-IL)**. He was especially adept in finding spy documents inside pumpkins, as in the Alger Hiss case.

Nixon served as **Eisenhower**'s two-term Vice-President, but was defeated in his first bid for the White House in 1960, by himself on television, and by Democrat John F. Kennedy in the narrowest Presidential election (to that time) in US history. Nixon's petulant arrogance made him an icon of all that was wrong with the idyllic, isolationist, know-nothing 1950s. He had a penchant for baring his narrow soul in public which was to stand him in ill stead throughout his public life. His hilarious "Checkers Speech", in which his wife, Patricia, sits stiffly beside him in her "good Republican cloth coat" as he defends their supposedly frugal lifestyle [and *yes,* he throws back at nameless accusers, they *do* have a dog, for his little daughters' enjoyment, and isn't that his right as an American??], is a classic of deception and disinformation.

Later, losing a bid to become Governor of California, Nixon blamed his loss on the **Media**, saying they "would not have Nixon to kick around anymore". Sadly, he did not keep his word, and returned to capture the Presidential nomination in 1968, promising to end the tragic Vietnam War. When wildly unpopular Democratic President Lyndon Johnson declined to seek a second term; Robert Kennedy, brother of the martyred JFK, was murdered moments after winning the California Democratic primary; and the Democratic Convention became a televised spectacle of Chicago's finest beating the bejeezus out of long-haired, anti-war, but still mostly White middle-class American youth, Nixon had a clear track to the Presidency.

XIII

Death

His eventual disengagement from Southeast Asia, and his historic 8-day visit to the People's Republic of China, in 1972, would have secured a favorable place in history for Nixon, had he not been caught up in a little burglary at Democratic National Headquarters that became known as *Watergate* (see *Card XVI*). Nixon was re-elected by a landslide in 1972, saying, "*I am not a crook*," but by the time televised hearings on Watergate ended, few believed him. An "unindicted co-conspirator" in the burglary, Nixon barely escaped impeachment, but resigned from office on August 9, 1974, the only US President so far to do so. He was issued a prompt Presidential pardon by his successor and second-term Vice President, **Gerald Ford**. Even after this appalling disgrace, however, Nixon didn't stay down. His continued importance to US-Chinese *detente*, his best-selling memoirs and well-attended lectures, fully "rehabilitated" the Burglar-President into elder statesman before his death.

Nixon signed into law the Endangered Species Act,[lxxxvii] thus providing succeeding Republican administrations with something to rail against and tear down.

On this card, gaunt *Death* carries a banner with the sign of Pisces, the two-faced, slippery one of the Zodiac, trampling all underfoot without regard for virtue or station, as in the "Saturday Night Massacre", the term given to Nixon's executive dismissal of independent special Watergate prosecutor Archibald Cox, and the forced resignations of Attorney General Elliot Richardson and Deputy Attorney General William Ruckelshaus, as the scandal unfolded. In the distance, the sun is setting – or rising – between the two towers, or elevators, which so often appear in our **Tarot**'s landscape; clearly, here as in *Card XVIII*, they represent the "ups and downs" of public life.

XIV
Time

Secretary of State for Presidents **Nixon** and **Ford**, close intellectual associate of former Vice President and New York Governor Nelson **Rockefeller** and his brother, David, and *sub rosa* foreign policy advisor to both **Bush** administrations, **Henry Kissinger** is our Angel of *Time*.

Kissinger, a German-born American diplomat, 1973 Nobel Peace Prize winner and proponent of *Realpolitik*, pioneered a policy of *détente* that led to relaxed US – Soviet relations. He played a crucial role in 1971 talks with Chinese Premier Zhou Enlai, leading to rapprochement between China and the US, and the formation of a new anti-Soviet alliance.

Kissinger cut a flamboyant figure, appearing at social events with sexy female celebrities. His foreign policy record made him enemies amongst the anti-war left and anti-Communist hawks on the right. With the declassification of Nixon and Ford administration documents relating to US policy in South America and East Timor, Kissinger has come under fire from human rights advocacy groups in the US and abroad. France, Brazil, Chile, Spain, and Argentina have sought to question him in connection with suspected war crimes such as Operation Condor, hindering his travel abroad.[lxxxviii]

In the card Waite calls *Temperance*, a winged angel, neither Hawk nor Dove, pours shining essences of compromise and political longevity between two chalices. The angel has one foot on dry land and one in the water, or, one in each camp. "Hereof is some part of the Secret of Eternal Life, as it is possible to man in his incarnation..."[lxxxix]

The Russian mystic Ouspensky writes, "One of the cups the angel holds is the past, the other is the future. The rainbow stream between the cups is the present. You see that it flows both ways. This is *Time* in its most incomprehensible aspect." Indeed, the unending influence of this German immigrant, more Vulture than Hawk or Dove, is incomprehensible to the common man, who does not perceive, Ouspensky continues, "that everything perpetually meets and that *Time* is a multitude of turning circles", and admonishes the trembling human Seeker to "listen and try to understand, for now understanding is your only salvation."[xc] *Time* has no mercy.

XIV

Time

XV
The Devil

The Evil One, former President/First Lady Billary, or the [first?] **Clinton Administration** (1993-2001), batwinged, crouches on the altar of Popularity. (Note resemblance to the Judeo-Christian *Devil* Belial.) A pentagram above the horned double head carries the Sign of the United Nations: *666*. One of the heads has business-length blonde hair; the other has recently been trimmed by an expensive Hollywood barber. A flabby gut overhangs garish running shorts, presenting a none-too-subtle image of sensual laxity. The right hand is raising a cheeseburger to its gaping maw; the left hand is slapping it down. One of his/her feet is wearing a high-heeled pump; the other is a chicken's foot.

Two acolytes, Bill Clinton's Attorney General, **Janet Reno**, and Vice President, **Al Gore** (clueless Democratic nominee in 2004 and 2007's Nobel Peace Prize Winner), are chained, even in their complaisance, to the altar. They are analogous to the *Lovers* of *Trump VI*, signifying Adam and Eve *after* the Fall. Behind Reno are the smoldering remains of the Branch Davidian compound in Waco, Texas; behind Gore, remaindered copies of his books. *Here is the downside of material power*. Tailed as they are, to show their animal nature, yet there is human intelligence in the faces of the acolytes; and even S/He who is exalted above them is not devoid of wit so much as disdainful of it.

This is also the card of Gemini, the astrologic Twins, the flip-flopping waffler, "*six of one, half a dozen of the other*". Many paranoid schizophrenics and bipolar manic-depressives are born in Gemini.

XV

The Devil

XVI
The Watergate

In most **Tarot**s, this card is designated *The Tower*. In French decks, it is *La Maison de Dieu*, or, "the house of God". I have chosen to re-name it for the event of the twentieth century which most changed both the image and the substance of the Republican Party: *Watergate*, as it became called in the verbal shorthand of the day, for the Republican-engineered and -bungled break-in and burglary of Democratic Party Headquarters in 1972 at the Watergate office building in Washington, DC. Originally denied, downplayed, and misrepresented by everyone involved, this relatively minor campaign espionage escapade, one of an extended agenda of "dirty tricks" to assure **Nixon**'s second term, instead brought down his Presidency, conceding the rest of the 1970's to Jimmy Carter's flaccid administration. A disaster of the highest order, the Watergate scandal saw thousands of loyal Republicans abandon the Party, and the squeaky-clean image cultivated and fervently supported by Party regulars dragged through the mud of months-long televised hearings featuring Republican-hired goons, *gusanos,* and brown-nosers. Very few White House intimates -- even those who were patently naïve stooges -- escaped the carnage.

Our card is illustrated in the traditional manner, as an imposing structure -- *the Party itself* -- rent by sudden lightning from a clear though darkling sky. Its roof is torn off; its inner workings revealed. Both bureaucrats and burglars are thrown from the wreckage.

The fire which leaps from several windows is, however, a cleansing fire; in the long run, the *Watergate* is a card of renewal. The old is destroyed to make way for the new. Once we have been deeply shocked by some egregious behavior on the part of our public officials, we are less shocked when it recurs. Without the mind-numbing *Watergate* affair, **Oliver North**'s campaign tactics twenty years later would have had greater consequences for the first **Bush** Administration. The card is a precursor of Darwin's principle of species adaptation through exposure to extreme conditions: whatever doesn't kill you makes you stronger.

XVI

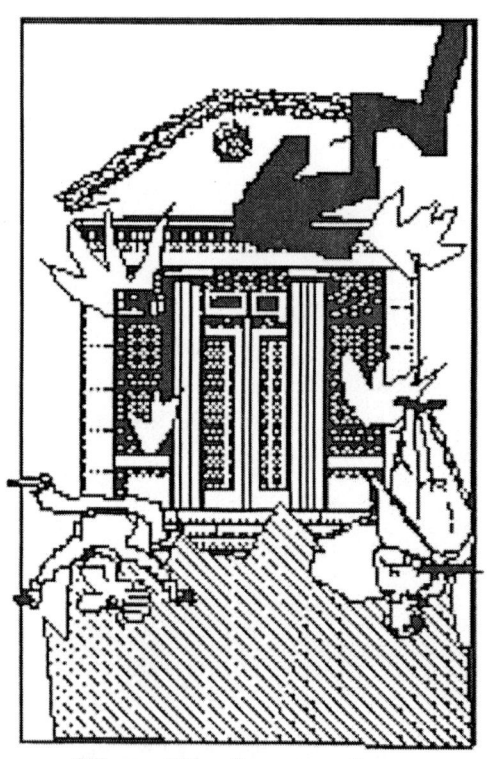

The Watergate

XVII
The Star

A great, radiant *Star* of eight rays[xci] is joined by logos of **Multinational Corporations**, "stars" of the modern economy. A naked female figure kneels on the land, one foot in the water. She pours Industrial Waste from two great vessels, polluting earth and sea. Nearby, a lonely songbird perches, wondering why its eggs won't hatch. This is the card of Aquarius, the Zodiacal water-carrier; as in, *"Rep. Feebler carries water for Worldwide Wasteland, Inc., on the Hill."*[xcii]

Republicans defend rampant Capitalism, holding that in Capital's growth lies betterment for all citizens. Yet confounding the precepts of an *economic system* with the *political* precepts of Democracy lets Capital run amok, giving to phrases such as *"the Almighty Dollar"* their *currency*. It is in the nature of Capital to *make profit*, without regard for national borders or human needs; and in the nature of Democracy to require a self-identified, loyal polity. Avoidance of overt clashes of these *competing systems* upon the shoals of Contradiction relies upon twin pillars (as so often in our text!) of Delusion and Cowardice. Thus, our once-spacious skies are poisoned with pollutants; our amber fields of grain have become reeking feedlots; our shining seas, sewers. Yet outcry at the desecration of our heritage is thought unseemly, and stifled in the folds of the Flag.

XVII

The Star

XVIII
The Moon

Former US Senator **Bob Packwood (R-OR)**, relieved of his Senatorial duties in 1995 after aggressive and unwanted advances to women in his office made him an embarrassment to all and sundry, appears as a jackass (not to be confused with the Democratic donkey), viewing the reflected *Moon* in a pond. In this card, **Political Sex Scandals**[xciii] represent the life of imagination versus the life of reality. A yellow brick road between two towers, or stiffies (Packwood's favorite place for romantic *tetes-a-tete* was Senate Building elevators), leads into the unknown. A dog wearing a bandanna howls mournfully beside the path. A crab-like creature, representing that nameless and hideous tendency which is lower than the savage beast, crawls up on the narrow beach. This is also the card for Cancer, birth sign of many perverts. It is associated, clearly, with the Moon itself, and the activity of "mooning"; some will also see a reflection of Uranus.

Waite says that the message of this card is, "*Peace, be still...*" We can only hope that he is right, and that the message is heeded, but *succeeding* scandals, such as those involving Rep. Mark Livingston (**R-LA**, resigned 1999); Rep. Henry Hyde (**R-IL**, who called his extramarital affair a "youthful indiscretion"); serial adulterer and Speaker of the House **Newt Gingrich (R-GA)**; adulterer Rep. Steve LaTourette (**R-OH**); chicken-hawking Rep. Edward Schrock (**R-VA**); allegedly abusive adulterer Don Sherwood (**R-PA**); and Rep Mark Foley (**R-FL**), of "Page-gate" notoriety, do not inspire optimism.[xciv]

XVIII

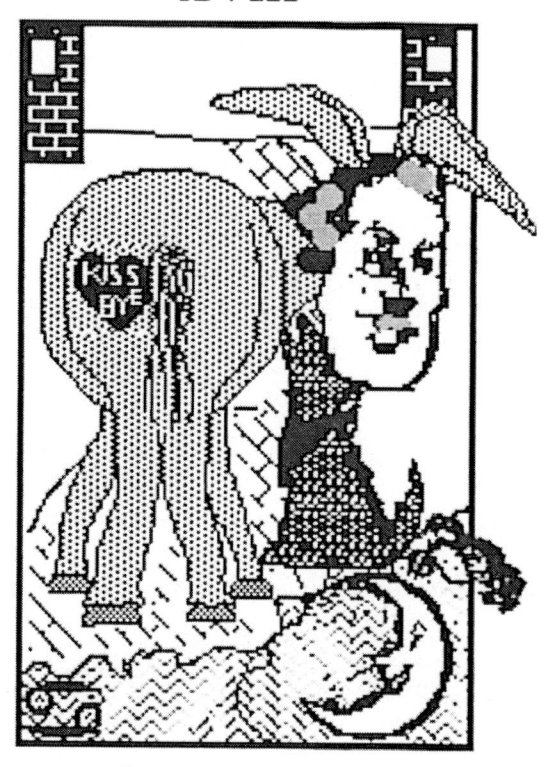

The Moon

XIX
The Sun

Shown in his moment of glory (1995), former Speaker of the House of Representatives **Newt Gingrich** (**R-PA**), buck nekkid, riding the Donkey of subjugated and complaisant Democrats (note that no spurs or reins are in evidence!) and waving the red banner of the "Contract with America", is the *Sun*, that great light which leads the endless procession of humanity, passing out of the walled garden of conservative think-tanks into the mainstream of History. This light is typified by the heart of a little child: impatient, greedy and self-important!

In May, 1988, Rep. Gingrich brought ethics charges against then-Speaker Jim Wright (**D-TX**), who had used a book deal to circumvent campaign finance and House rules, and who resigned as a result. Gingrich's success in forcing Wright out added to his influence. In 1989, Minority Whip **Cheney** became Secretary of Defense, and Gingrich succeeded him as Whip. After the Republican victory in 1994, he became Speaker.

Spiritual kin to Radical Republicans who sought to reform the chastened Confederacy with fire and brimstone, Gingrich and an eager horde of freshman legislators, fondly referred to as "the Hezbollah" by their more seasoned colleagues, tried to enforce the judgmental piety of what became commonly called "the contract *on* America".

Gingrich was himself accused of unethical behavior when he accepted an advance *as part of a book deal*. Eighty-four ethics charges were filed against him, and he was fined $300,000 after the House Ethics Committee concluded that his use of tax-deductible money for political purposes, and the inaccurate information he supplied to investigators, represented "intentional or . . . reckless" disregard of the rules[xcv]

In 2007, it was reported that Gingrich was having an extramarital affair at the same time he was leading the charge against then-President Bill **Clinton** over *his* tawdry involvement with White House intern Monica Lewinsky; however, Gingrich did not feel he had been hypocritical. Long a proponent of making English the "official language" of the US, and an opponent of bilingual education, Gingrich was reported considering a Presidential run in 2008 until reports of growing voter **Diversity** put a damper on his plans.

XIX

The Sun

XX
The Supreme Court

In this longed-for scene of Republican Rapture, an Angel, surrounded by clouds and blowing a trumpet, announces the Second Coming of a Conservative Majority on the High Court. From the marble halls which have been the tomb of much strict constructionist argument, nine robed Justices arise.

The **2007 Roberts Court** may come close to meeting Republican hopes, with strong pro-business rulings despite ideological differences in other areas. The court has issued rulings which have made it harder to sue companies for securities fraud and antitrust violations, and shielded businesses from large consumer damage awards. One consumer advocate said, "This court looks at big companies as its clients, rather than the citizens of the United States."[xcvi] The banner depending from the Angel's trumpet is blazoned with the dollar sign.

Waite says that this card, styled conventionally as *The Last Judgment*, "registers the accomplishment of the great work of transformation..."[xcvii] When the Roll is called Up Yonder, who will be confirmed?

XX

The Supreme Court

XXI
The World

The same party animals of the Apocalypse which encircled *Trump X, the Wheel of Fortune,* are seen here: the uniformed enforcer of material society, the ostrich of isolation, the dried bones of entrenched interests, and the grinning feline of predatory greed. In the center an Elephant, symbol of the Greedy Old Party itself, draped in red velvet ribbon, here denotes **Republican Victory**. Red, white and blue bunting encircles the beast, while the Grand Old Flag drapes it, protecting it from harmful innuendo. On a deeper level, the card represents the Rapture of the Universe when it knows itself within G-d, or the state of the soul when conscious of Divine Vision reflected by self-knowing intelligence, or that Sublime Moment just before blacking out at the open bar Victory Party at the winner's hotel! Being in harmony with Divine Vision can have no outcome other than success.

XXI

The World

0
The Fool

Self-made Texas jillionaire and loose-cannon-Presidential spoiler (1992; 1996) **H. Ross Perot** struts along a cliff edge, the two-party system as we know it. He must believe in a Flat Earth! He has enough *Coins* in his bag to do whatever he wants, and enough *chutzpah* to do it, *especially* if it harelips the dull little beancounters. Also in his bag are other tools of *Magick*: simplistic solutions, an aggressive demeanor, *Soldier of Fortune* magazine. He wears the face of Underdog. A bullfrog, representing his folksy line of bullcrap, accompanies him along the precipice. The card is associated with Taurus, the Zodiac's symbol of bullheadedness.

After Navy service, Perot was a salesman for IBM. He became a top producer, and tried to pitch his own ideas to his bosses, but was ignored. He left IBM to found Electronic Data Systems (EDS). He was refused 88 times before he got one contract. He won lucrative contracts from the US government in the 1960s. When EDS went public, its stock went from $16 a share to $160 in days. Just before the 1979 Iranian Revolution, the government there imprisoned two of Perot's employees in a contract dispute. He hired a rescue team led by a retired Special Forces colonel. When the team couldn't extract the two hostages, they waited for pro-Ayatollah revolutionaries to storm the jail and free all 10,000 inmates. The EDS employees were met by the team and spirited out of Iran. The exploit is recounted in Ken Follett's book, *On Wings of Eagles*.

A little later, Texas Governor Bill Clements asked Perot's help to reduce illegal drug use in the state. Perot led a **War on Drugs** Committee that proposed five repressive new laws, all of which were passed. In 1982, Clements asked him to improve the states' schools, and he led major reform efforts. Under the best known of these, the "no pass, no play" rule, students must have passing grades to play sports. This overthrew a long Texas tradition of scholastic neglect of ath-a-leets. In the 1992 Presidential election, Perot received 18.9% of the popular vote, the most successful Independent run since **Theodore Roosevelt**'s in 1912. Some analysts say Perot was a spoiler in the election, drawing votes away from **George W. Bush** and allowing **Bill Clinton** to win. Perot was entitled to federal election funding in 1996. He remained in the public eye by opposing the **North American Free Trade Agreement**, urging voters to listen for the "giant sucking sound" as American jobs headed south, should NAFTA be ratified.[xcviii]

0

The Fool

§ 3
THE GREATER ARCANA AND THEIR DIVINATORY MEANINGS

1. THE MAGICIAN. — Self-confidence. Will meets skill. Initiative. Flexible, dexterous, a good dancer (for such a heavy man). Capability. Technology, innovation. *Reversed:* Misleading deception. Cunning, guile, trickery. Manipulation. Propaganda all is phony. Mass hallucination. Science ruled by superstition. Dinosaurs in Biblical days. Shock jocks.

2. THE HIGH PRIESTESS. — Wisdom. Therapy. Rehabilitation. Twelve steps. Perhaps, recovery. Serenity prayer. Learning. Common sense. Understanding. Woman in her Aspect as Co-Dependent. *Reversed:* Demanding. Hidden emotion, reserve. Coldness. Addiction; mental and physical illness. Impatience. Selfishness. Blaming bad actions on alcohol, drugs, or one's unhappy childhood and terrible parents.

3. THE EMPRESS. — Action. Development. Marriage; family values. Mother, sister, wife. Power behind the throne. Influence through suggestion. Woman in Her Aspect as Mommy. *Reversed:* Tears. Feminine wiles. Controversial advisors. Spendthrift. Nagging. Eating one's young. Naming names to the Committee. Just Say 'No'.

4. THE EMPEROR. — Worldly power. Wealth, box office appeal. Stability. Authority. Family values; father, brother, husband. Endurance, longevity. Popular leader. *Reversed:* Insularity. Shallowness. Lies. Inconsideration. Arrogance. Firing striking federal air traffic controllers. Dead hand on the throttle. "Reaganomics".

5. THE DUFFER. — Mercy. Pardon, a reprieve. A deal. Good advice. Good lie. Inspiration. Alliance. Humility. Bag-man. *Reversed:* Servitude. Inactivity. Timidity. Captivity. Clumsy, awkward. Lack of conviction, as in, "the jury is still out." Unrealistic beliefs.

6. THE LOVERS. — Young love. Beauty. Harmony. Unanimity, togetherness. Trials overcome. Confidence. Trust. True romance. Revenge of the nerds. Who else would date them? *Reversed:* Temptation. Over-optimism. Oblivious to possible consequences; cluelessness. Social inbreeding.

7. THE CHARIOT. — War. Revenge. Trouble approaching. Conflicting influences. Uncontrolled outside powers; lobbyists. Turmoil. Parting of the Red Sea. Indecision. Perplexity. Chaos. *Reversed:* Triumph. Conquest. A voyage.

8. JUSTICE. — Equity, fairness. Reasonableness, proper balance. Harmony. Virtue, honor. Virginity before marriage. Just rewards.

Reversed: Self-righteous smugness.; self-justification. Gossip. Good intentions pave the road to Hell. Airing dirty laundry. Woman in Her Aspect as Shrew.

9. THE HERMIT. — Prudence. Circumspection. Treason, rogues, corruption. A loner with three first names is stalking you! *Reversed:* Recession, backsliding. Concealment, disguise; obscurity. Neither policy-making nor sausage-making should be observed. "The truth is out there somewhere."

10. THE ELECTORAL PROCESS. — Destiny. Dame Fortune, Lady Luck. Approaching change. Perpetual motion. The flux of human affairs. Fate. Culmination. Nearing an answer or a conclusion. Heads, I win. *Reversed:* Tails, you lose. The *Wheel* is fixed; the House always wins.

11. STRENGTH. — Defiance, zeal, fervor. Physical power, muscle. Energy. Determination, resolution. Courage. Promises. Distractions. *Reversed:* Mind games, propaganda. Affirmative action. UFOs, alien abduction. US-trained terrorists. A load of fertilizer. Misdirection.

12. THE HANGED MAN. — Sacrifice. Renunciation. Surrender, self-abandonment. Suspension. Gravity boots. Abeyance of self-interest. Comatose. Triangles. The Tax Code. *Reversed:* Indecision, lack of progress. Readjustment. Seen and unseen outside factors wield a strong influence. More triangles. I'd like to buy a vowel, please!

13. DEATH. — Sudden change. Surprising, unexpected. Making it perfectly clear. The end. Permanent ego damage from being kicked around. The Five O'clock Shadow knows! *Reversed:* Partial rebirth. Beginnings. Deep influences.

14. TIME. — Appeasement, accommodation, affinity, management, moderation. Sleight of hand, obfuscation. Recycled policies. *Reversed:* Disunion, unfortunate juxtapositions, conflicting interests. Self-justifying.

15. THE DEVIL. — Evil incarnate and triumphant. Corrupt powers. Flexible morals. Secular humanism. Prevarication. Gays in the military; draft-dodging; federal abortion mills; welfare Cadillacs; affirmative action. (From *Arkansas,* of all places; my *G-d;* at least the Carters were *civilized!*) *Reversed:* Subordination. Downfall. Dependency upon others. Semen stains on a blue dress. OR, a ball-cutting, pants-wearing woman who speaks with forked tongue.

16. THE WATERGATE. — Disruption. Adversity. Calamity. Shock and awe. Caught in the act! Rocked foundations, rats deserting a sinking ship. Ruin. Bankruptcy. *Reversed:* Events now left behind. Separating the wheat from the chaff. Survival of the fittest. New directions.

17. THE STAR. — Hope. Satisfaction. Bright prospects. Shipping manifest; destiny. New horizons. Rewards of hard work; golden

parachute. Headquarters in Dubai. *Reversed:* Easily influenced. A swindle; pillage of retirement funds. Pollution of the deeps. Selling past and present for a dubious future. Surveyors and real estate developers. Big box stores and ticky-tacky condos in *your* neighborhood. Shifting sands of loyalty.

    18. THE MOON. — Scandal. Error. Disillusionment. Public embarrassment. Bad influence. Kiddie porn; sexual predator. Insincerity. Selfishness. *Reversed:* Caution. Do not pass 'Go' if she says 'No'! Don't blame the booze!

    19. THE SUN. — Triumph, victory. Happiness, devotion. Accomplishment. Warmth, sincerity. Absolutely no shame. The true believer. *Reversed:* Burn-out, melt-down, freak-out. Over-exposure. Blinded by one's own light. Divorce. Family embarrassment; in Charades, "sounds like *thespian blister* ...."

    20. THE SUPREME COURT. — Determination, decision. Result, outcome. Readjustment. Opportunity knocking; time to reinvest in insurance stocks. Limitation of corporate liability. *Reversed:* Atonement, repentance, apology. A three million dollar cup of hot coffee. The pendulum swings.

    21. THE WORLD. — Completion. Perfection. Synthesis. Success. Assurance. Control of both houses of Congress. *A strongly favorable card signifying a positive outcome in any position.*

    Zero. THE FOOL. — Thoughtlessness. Extravagance. Lack of discipline. Not a team player. Folly, unrestrained frenzy. Careless promises. A little knowledge is a dangerous thing; a few bricks shy of a load. *Reversed:* New beginning. Adventure, excitement, corporate commando raids. On the cutting edge, and twisting it in your back!

PART III

The Outer Method of the Oracles

§ 1
Distinction Between the Greater and Lesser Arcana

It is generally agreed-upon that the 56 cards of the Lesser Arcana do not carry any of the deep philosophical significance of the preceding twenty-two Trumps Major, or Greater Arcana, but are at root mere adornments, which may receive various interpretations depending upon their suites, order, and the mythical properties of numbers. Indeed, there is no reason to fault this view. It is also commonly agreed that modern playing cards are directly descended from the Lesser Arcana, particularly adapted to the common pursuits of gaming, but useful as well for simple "fortune-telling".

Why, then, do all versions of the tarot persist in ascribing detailed symbols and meanings to these 56 lesser cards, so far beyond the strictly necessary suit and number?

Why, for three reasons, and three alone: *in the first place*, as creative expressions of the individual artists who envision various complex and well-imagined tarot sets; *in the second place*, and with the **Republican Tarot** in particular, because Iniquity and Fortune have each a thousand faces, and government is not always met in high matters of State, but all too often in petty and annoying episodes, and thus it shall be seen in many of the cards which follow; *and in the third place*, and lastly, Gentle Reader, because the prospect of 79 oddly amusing plates in a book, or 79 unique cards in a colorful deck, is much more likely to part you from your hard-earned *Coins* than a tarot made up of 22 Greater Arcana alone!

Through the unnerving and ambiguous images dredged up in the following section, then, let us forge ahead into the lower, and more sordid, reaches of the **Republican Tarot!**

§ 2.
THE LESSER ARCANA

Otherwise, the Four Suites of Tarot Cards.

Suite of Bushes.

BUSHES
Player

George Herbert Walker Bush, 41st President (1989-1993), the first president with four names, was 43rd Vice-President under **Reagan**, a US Congressman (**R-TX**), and Ambassador to the United Nations. He is the only President to have directed the Central Intelligence Agency, or led a diplomatic mission to China.[xcix] His father, Prescott Bush,[c] was a US Senator (**R-ME**). Bush is the oldest living former President at this time.

The only World War II combat aviator President and the last of six President-veterans of that war, he was commissioned before age 19, the youngest Naval aviator at that time. In 1944, his plane was hit. He and a crew member bailed out. The other man's parachute didn't open, and he fell to his death. Anti-**Drug Warriors** know that the parachute cords which saved Bush were made of cannabis hemp, but none say with what the other fellow's chute was tied!

After the war, Bush led the Yale baseball team to the first College World Series. Like his Dad, he joined Skull and Bones. After graduation, he became a Texas oilman, working for a subsidiary of Brown Brothers Harriman, where Papa Bush was a Director.

In 1964, Bush ran for US Senate against Ralph Yarborough (**D-TX**), who called Bush a "tool of eastern kingmakers". Bush lost, but in 1966 was elected to the US House and assigned to the powerful Ways and Means Committee. In 1970, Bush again challenged Yarborough. He won the Republican primary, but Lloyd Bentsen[ci] beat Yarborough for the Democratic nod, then defeated Bush. **Nixon** was re-elected President and named Bush to chair the Republican National Committee, just as *Watergate* broke. In 1976, **Ford** named Bush CIA Director. Bush called the appointment "a shocker" and denied prior agency involvement.[cii] The choice was opposed by some. After Bush pledged not to run for office in

Player of Bushes

1976, the opposition faded. Democrats took power instead in '76, and Bush went to work for a Houston bank.

Reagan and Bush won in 1980 and 1984. In Bush's second term as Veep, he was the first to be Acting President, for about 8 hours, mostly spent playing tennis. When the **Iran-Contra affair** broke, Bush said he'd been "out of the loop", unaware of illegal arms or cocaine sales. When he won the Oval Office in 1988, he invaded Panama, deposing former doubles partner Gen. Noriega.[ciii]

On 9/11, **1990**, he said: "*Out of these troubled times, our fifth objective — a New World Order — can emerge: a new era.*" At first believed to be a new professional wrestling association, Bush's "N.W.O." has proven even more choreographed. When Iraqi leader Saddam Hussein, another US-armed tyrant, invaded oil-rich Kuwait, the UN opposed him, fearing he might invade Saudi Arabia. The first **Iraq** (a.k.a. Gulf) **War** ended quickly, leaving Hussein in power, a legacy enemy for First Son **George W**. Papa Bush didn't oust Hussein because, "*We would have had to occupy Baghdad and... rule Iraq*". Indeed we would.

He lost in 1992 after raising taxes despite pledging ("*Read my lips: no new taxes*") not to do so. His last official act was pardoning former Secretary of Defense Caspar Weinberger, charged with lying to Congress about Iran-Contra and his talks with other officials about illegal arms sales. Pardon may have prevented Bush's own appearance before a grand jury.

In 2006, activists charged Bush I with war crimes in Panama and Iraq. These were filed, for some labyrinthine reason, in Iceland, where response has been predictably cool.[civ]

The former President works for The Carlyle Group, government defense contractors. Investors include his good friends, the Saudi Arabian bin Laden family.

Divinatory Meanings: Unexpected inheritance. Dynastic dreams. Devotion. *Reversed:* Dogma hit by karma. Careerism. Secrets revealed. Pretension. A Japanese verb, "*bushuru*", means "to commit public vomiting; to do [a] Bush".

BUSHES

Lady

Barbara Pierce Bush, Lady of the Bush suite, has written several books attributed to various family dogs, demonstrating her metaphysical inclinations. She has a motherly mien, most fortunate since at least three of her offspring are among those only a mother could love. **George H.W.** and Barbara Bush had six children: Pauline, **George W.**, **Jeb**, **Neil**, Marvin, and Dorothy. Wife of one globally-inclined President and mother of another, she is herself best known for advocating literacy, which passes for wild-eyed idealism in *Bush* family circles. She has been candid about "the effort... she had to put in to help one of her sons... with his learning disability",[cv] however, it has never been entirely clear to which of her sons she refers. Her motherly instincts seem, however, confined to her own family. Two days before the second **Iraq War** was launched by son George W., she told ABC's *Good Morning, America,* "*Why should we hear about body bags and deaths? Oh, I mean, it's not relevant. So why should I waste my beautiful mind on something like that?*" While visiting a Houston relief center for people displaced by Hurricane Katrina in 2005, Mrs. Bush told the radio program *Marketplace*, "*Almost everyone I've talked to says, 'We're gonna move to Houston.' What I'm hearing, which is sort of scary, is they all want to stay in Texas... Everybody is so overwhelmed by the hospitality, and so many of the people in the arenas here, you know, were underprivileged anyway. This is working very well for them.*"

John Nichols of *The Nation* wrote, "Mrs. Bush chuckles audibly as she observes just how great things are going for families that are separated from loved ones, people who have been forced to abandon their homes and the only community where they have ever lived, and parents who are explaining to children that their pets, their toys and in some cases their friends may be lost forever."[cvi]

In 2006, it was learned that Barbara Bush donated money to the **Bush-Clinton** Katrina Fund on the condition the charity do business with an educational software company owned by third son **Neil**.[cvii]

Divinatory Meanings: Sympathetic. Charming. Worthy. *Reversed:* Insular, shallow. Terrible taste in men.

Lady of Bushes

BUSHES
Knave

"**George Walker Bush**... 43rd... President... the eldest son of former... President **George H. W. Bush**... was elected... in... 2000... [and] re-elected in 2004...

"Bush worked in his family's oil businesses following college. In 1978, he made an unsuccessful run for [US Congress]. He later co-owned the Texas Rangers... He... was elected Governor of Texas in 1994...",[cviii] perhaps to get him away from Arlington; however, the Rangers continued to stumble, and have still never been to a World Series.

"[I]n 2000... Bush lost the national popular vote and the **Supreme Court** decision in *Bush* v. *Gore* stopped a recount in **Florida**, preserving Bush's 537-vote margin" there, providing his winning electoral votes.

"As President, Bush pushed through a $1.3 trillion tax cut... the *No Child Left Behind Act*[cix] and has... pushed for... the Partial-Birth **Abortion** Ban Act and faith-based **Welfare** initiatives.

"After... September 11, 2001, Bush declared a global *War on Terrorism* and [invaded] Afghanistan to overthrow the Taliban, destroy Al-Qaeda and to capture Osama bin Laden... In March 2003, [he] ordered the **Iraq** invasion, asserting that Iraq [had weapons of mass destruction, violating a UN ban], and that the war was necessary [to protect] the [US].

"Running as a... 'war president'... Bush's... re-election... campaign... was successful despite controversy over... the... War and... the economy... After his re-election, Bush received increasing... criticism, even from former allies. His domestic approval... declined from 90 [%]... immediately after... September 11, 2001... to 26 [%] ... in June 2007), the lowest level for any sitting President in 35 years."[cx]

I have parsed the **Wikipedia** entry for George "Dubya" Bush at such length because, from here in the midst of his second administration, it is truly impossible to see which of his blunders and egregious acts History will most condemn. Yet what can be seen is the devolution of a dynasty, from self-made robber barons and war profiteers to silver-spoonfed,

Knave of Bushes

spoiled brats. "*I am the Deciderer!*" Bush II proclaims – yet Bush I's enemies, friends, advisors, and the wet dreams of international dealmakers define him. Shown on a galloping horse in a desert land, oblivious to its ancient monuments, the Knave of Bushes has no exit strategy. In our deck, he is the One-Eyed Jack; and we may well recall, as our civil liberties are mangled beyond recognition under cover of the never-ending "war on terror", that "*in the land of the blind, the one-eyed man is King.*"

Divinatory Meanings: Change of residence, emigration, forced removal. Precipitate departure. *Reversed:* Quixotic. Rupture, division, discord. A 10-gallon hat on a 2-quart head.

BUSHES
Varlet

In a classic pose of young Texans of their generation, **Neil Mallon Bush** and **John Ellis "Jeb" Bush**, third and second sons, respectively, of **George H.W.** and **Barbara**, kid brothers of **George W.**, pose astride a paint horse. Their bland, featureless, sunny surroundings reflect the essential rootlessness of a family which lived in 17 different cities and 29 houses as they were growing up.[cxi]

Jeb, 43rd Governor of **Florida** (1999-2007), may someday run for Senate, or even for President, but since leaving office has concentrated on an earlier ambition. "*I want to be very wealthy*", he said when his father was Vice-President. In pursuit of that goal, Jeb worked in real estate and for a cel phone company, was on the Board of a Norwegian group which sold equipment for the Alaska oil pipeline, owned a shoe company in Panama, got involved in a scheme to sell water pumps in Nigeria, and worked for Cuban exile Miguel Recarey, who had earlier aided the CIA in its attempts to assassinate Cuban Premier Fidel Castro. In 1990, Jeb prevailed upon his Dad to pardon notorious, unrepentant anti-Castro terrorist Orlando Bosch.[cxii] Jeb was Governor during the disputed 2000 Presidential elections, which brother George won by the narrowest of margins only after a **Supreme Court** decision halting a recount of the Florida vote, where many documented, outrageous efforts to intimidate and disenfranchise elderly and black voters perceived to favor the Democratic candidate, Al Gore, had taken place. Jeb's Secretary of State, Katherine Harris, was widely criticized and ridiculed for her role in the voting fiasco, but in the end, the Florida vote was successfully stolen.

Jeb Bush is the first Governor to serve while a sibling was simultaneously President. When he was elected in 1999, brother George won his second term as Governor of Texas; they were then the first siblings to govern two states simultaneously since Nelson and Winthrop **Rockefeller** led New York and Arkansas, respectively (1967-1971).

Neil, the third son, has never held public office, but has influenced the education of almost every US public school child during George's terms in office due to the "*No Child Left Behind*" educational initiative, which apparently depended on computer software available only from Neil's

Varlets of Bushes

company, Ignite! Learning. Neil first came to national attention when, as a director, he OK'd loans at Silverado Savings and Loan which caused the thrift to fail in 1988, at a cost to taxpayers of $1.3 billion. Neil paid $50,000 in a settlement. A couple of ugly divorces later, he's selling the software almost all states use to determine if high school graduates have been minimally educated.

Oddly, while Jeb converted to Catholicism when he married Columba Gallo,[cxiii] it is Neil who served on the original board of a mysterious Swiss ecumenical foundation, along with then-Cardinal Ratzinger (later Pope Benedict XVI), the former chief rabbi of France, Jordan's Prince Hassan, another prominent Muslim, a religious scholar, a Greek Orthodox leader, and Neil's business partner.[cxiv] It seems more likely that this group was seeking the original stone tablets of the Ten Commandments than that its aims were remotely connected to anything which has been publicly stated. Neil may have lost interest when he learned that *Indiana Jones* is a fictional character!

In another totally weird twist, the family of John W. Hinckley, Jr., who tried to assassinate **Ronald Reagan** in 1981, made large contributions to then-Vice President George H.W. Bush's campaign chest. Before the assassination attempt, Hinckley's brother had been scheduled to have dinner, on what turned out to be the night following the fateful evening, at Neil and Sharon Bush's Denver home, accompanying one of Sharon's friends. Dinner was indefinitely postponed.[cxv]

Divinatory Meanings: An envoy, messenger. A spy. Loyalty. Family traits. *Reversed:* "Ride a painted pony, let the spinnin' wheel spin." Bad news.

Bushes
Ten

A plodding figure carries a load of ten *Bushes*, the **Middle-Class Tax Burden**, in this interpretation of a traditional design. The *Bushes* appear to be enclosed in a large, heavy bag, but we can see through it. The figure carrying the bag appears perplexed, and it is unclear where he is carrying his load, or for what purpose.

Divinatory Meanings: Oppression. Excessive pressure. Falsity. Disguise. If a lawsuit is involved, certain loss. *Reversed:* Duplicity. Treachery. A traitor. Deceiver. "No new taxes." Some losses will occur.

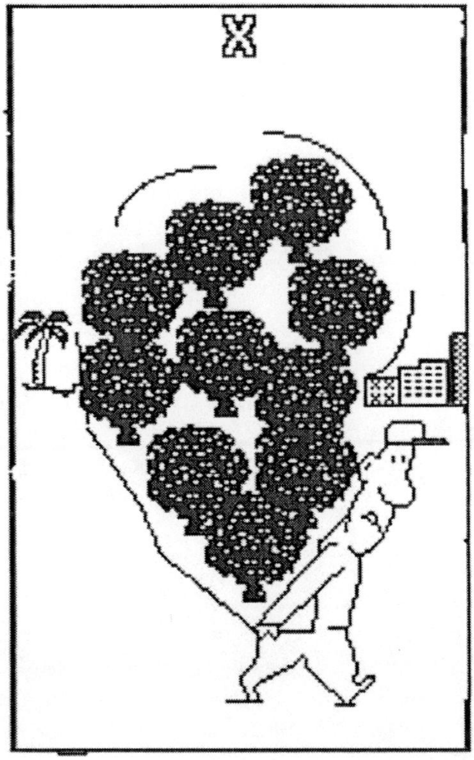
X

BUSHES
Nine

A sneering **Oliver North** holds a *Bush* tightly and awaits his enemies. Behind him are eight other *Bushes*, like a fence or palisade; perhaps the same ones seen in *Card VII* of this suite.

Col. North, a graduate of the US Naval Academy, was a career Marine officer. For service in Vietnam, he was awarded a Silver Star, Bronze Star, and two **Purple Heart**s.

"Ollie" came to national attention during the **Iran-Contra Affair**, when he was a key **Reagan** official involved in the clandestine sale of weapons to Iran, generating funds to support the Nicaraguan Contra rebels, in violation of US law. Vice Admiral John Poindexter and North, possibly without informing Reagan, diverted millions of dollars to the Contras from a secret deal which did have Reagan's approval: sales of anti-tank and anti-aircraft missiles to Iran, violating his public pledge not to deal with Iran's fanatic Ayatollah.

North's partners in laundering the Contra funds were associates of then-Vice President **George H.W. Bush**. North told Poindexter, "You will recall that over the years Manuel Noriega in Panama and I have developed a fairly good relationship," explaining that if US officials helped Noriega "clean up his image", and lifted the ban on arms sales to his Panamanian Defense Force, Noriega will "'take care of' the Sandinista leadership for us." North proposed paying the Panamanian dictator a million dollars from the Iranian arms sales for his help, as a gratuity.

North was tried in 1988 on 16 felony counts and initially convicted of accepting an illegal tip (Span.: *propina*) himself, aiding and abetting the obstruction of a congressional inquiry, and destruction of documents. He was given a suspended prison term, two years probation, $150,000 in fines, and 1200 hours community service. However, in 1990, with the help of the American Civil Liberties Union, his convictions were overturned, because he had been granted limited immunity for his testimony, and that testimony was deemed to have influenced witnesses at his trial.[cxvi]

Divinatory Meanings: Confrontation. Strength in opposition. *Reversed:* Obstacles, adversity, calamity. Disaster. Snafu.

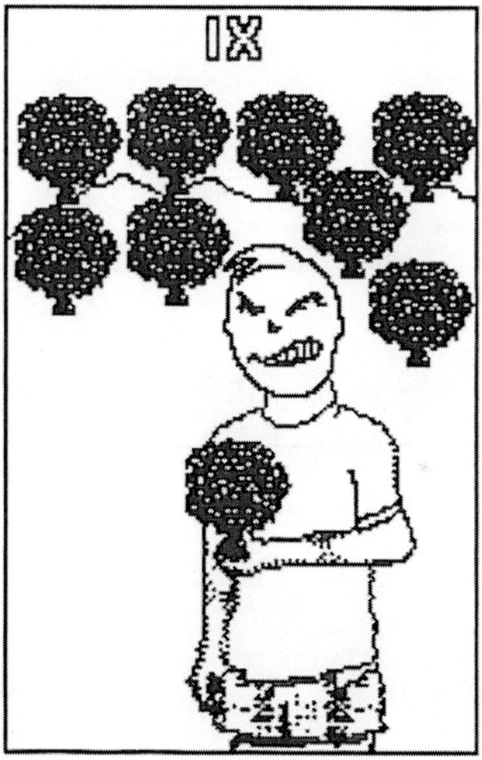
IX

Bushes
Eight

Salvage Logging in a traditional design. Eight *Bushes* in an old growth forest on national parkland lie clear-cut, destined to become particle board and tissue paper. Smokey the Bear warns the American public against forest fires; but whoever thought up "salvage sales" was a *genius!*

Divinatory Meanings: Swiftness. Activity towards an assured legislative end. Hasty decisions. The last forest primeval. Arrows of love; disposable chopsticks for the Asian market. *Reversed:* Jealousy, dispute. Harassment. Domestic violence. Environmental tree-hugging protesters. Stings of conscience; the ghost of **Teddy Roosevelt**.

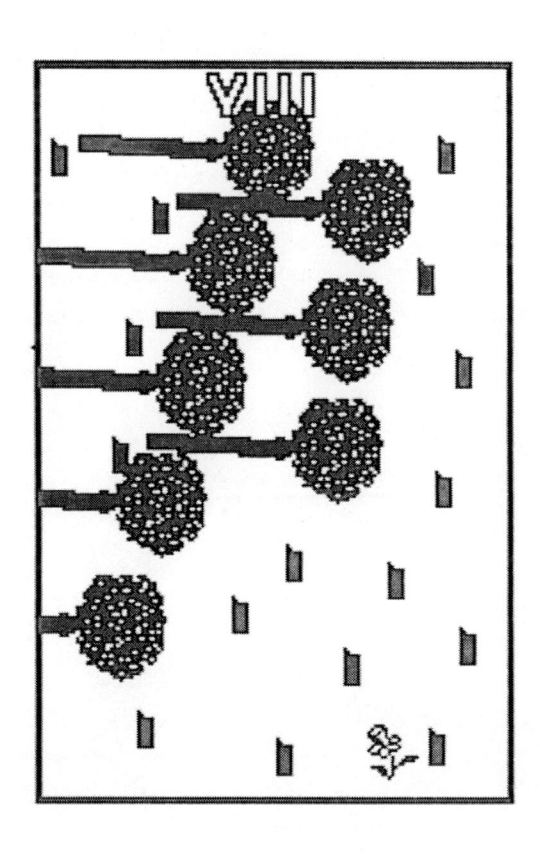

VIII

BUSHES
Seven

In Waite's *Tarot*, the youth in this card, holding one Wand aloft, fends off six Wands below, but I do not share this view. Instead it appears that a fence or palisade of *Bushes* is being built here – perhaps the same one seen, in maturity, in *Card IX* of this suite and, again, perhaps not – and whether to keep someone -- or something -- in, or out, no one can say. The youth is called **Homeland Security**, and where he sees a line drawn in the sand, others see only a river.

Whether the Seeker is faced with the consequences and outgrowths of "free trade" (the new *l'aissez faire*), an immigration policy wavering between porous borders and physical fences, or the growing irrelevancy of US citizens for ought but our bottomless consumerism – all among "globalization's" faces – let us not forget that these are economic issues, at root, and that *following the money* brings understanding.

Divinatory Meanings: Success, advantage. Courage. Spirited discussion; debate; negotiation. Trade wars. Surmountable obstacles. It furthers one to cross the river. *Reversed:* Embarrassed, anxious. Terrorists in flight school; strip searches at airports. Consternation, perplexity, corruption. Warning against indecision.

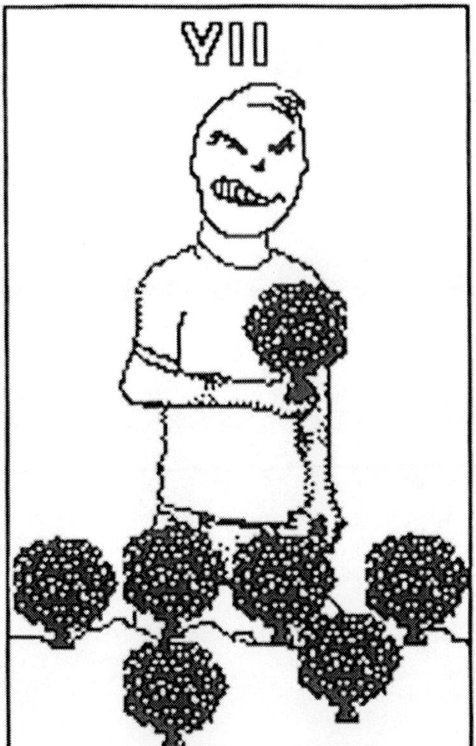
VII

BUSHES
Six

A controlling interest in the Family Channel is owned by televangelist Pat Robertson, who unsuccessfully sought the 1988 Republican Presidential nomination. In 1996, the San Diego convention bureau paid over $1.3 million to Robertson's cable channel for "special coverage" of the Republican National Convention there,[cxvii] although *free, gavel-to-gavel* coverage was being provided by the non-profit cable news network of record, C-SPAN. In well-brokered Republican infighting, sometimes losers win more than winners! The influence of the **Christian Right**, or *Moral Majority*, led by Robertson, Jerry Falwell, Jim and **Tammy Faye Bakker**, and others with a direct line to the Almighty, has been a mixed blessing for Republicans, attracting the faithful to candidates and positions anointed by these leaders, but creating a less forgiving, more cohesive, lower-rent "base" than Republicans are wont to succor.

Here, the seemingly Elect of G-d parades in an admiring throng, shaded by six *Bushes*, riding the familiar ostrich of isolationism, perhaps towards **Victory**, perhaps an embarrassing **Sex Scandal**.

Divinatory Meanings: Expected victory. Advancement. School prayer. Important news. Ignoring the beam in one's own eye in order to point out a mote in one's neighbor's. *Reversed:* Apprehension, fear. Illusion. Pearly Gates opened to the Enemy. Indefinite delay in the Rapture.

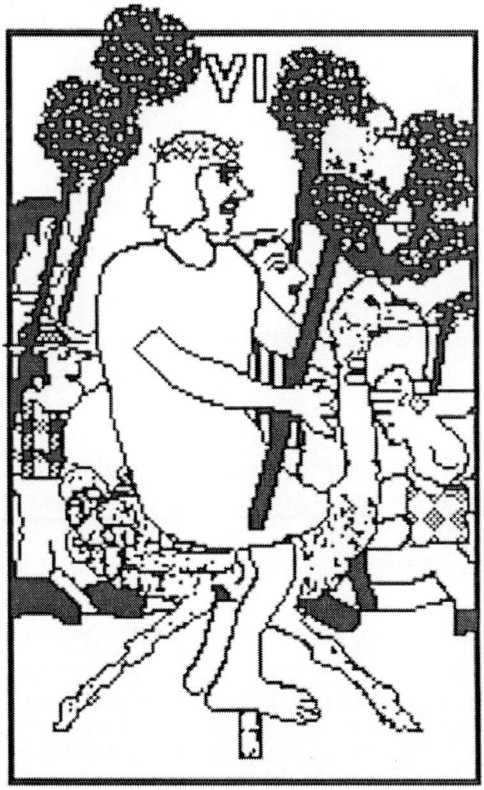
VI

BUSHES
Five

Five figures with long-stemmed *Bushes* thrash about in a free-for-all. They represent law enforcement, Native Americans, athletes, the chronically ill, and drug peddlers (legal and illegal). The card is the **War on Drugs**, declared by **Richard Nixon** and waged by every succeeding President and Congress upon the people. The War on Drugs is not directed against drugs, if one considers aspirin, antidepressants, and sexual potency-enhancing pills to be "drugs"; but against the use of any medicine or consciousness-altering substance not controlled and taxed by the government: patented, copyrighted, *owned*, and therefore *profited from*, by some large corporation.

Cannabis, the largest cash crop in the US, outpaces corn and wheat together. Domestic pot production increased ten-fold from 1980 -- 2005, from 2.2 million pounds to 22 million pounds, with an estimated annual value of $36 billion. It is the top cash crop in 12 states and worth more than $1 billion annually in five: California, Tennessee, Kentucky, Hawaii, and Washington.[cxviii]

US drug policies have not reduced illicit drug use or availability in America, while undermining human rights and destabilizing democracy abroad, particularly in Latin America, according to the nonprofit Washington Office on Latin America (WOLA). Retail prices for illicit drugs, specifically cocaine and heroin, have fallen dramatically even though government spending to reduce supply and demand has climbed. The number of drug offenders jailed in the US rose from approximately 45,000 in 1981 to over 480,000 in 2002. [cxix]

Since 1997, over a dozen prescription drugs approved by the federal Food and Drug Administration, which continues to ignore studies of marijuana's safety and benefits, have been taken off the market due to serious side effects -- in some cases after hundreds of injuries and even deaths.[cxx] Americans spend $200 billion a year on legal prescription drugs, a figure growing at about 12% a year. Drugs are the fastest-growing part of health care costs. Increases in drug spending reflect, almost equally, that we are taking more drugs than in the past; that they are more likely to be expensive new drugs than older, cheaper ones; and that the prices of heavily prescribed drugs are routinely raised, often several times a year.[cxxi]

V

In Afghanistan, where almost all of the world's heroin-producing poppies are grown, the crop was cultivated in only three provinces before US occupation of the country brought supposedly more stringent eradication programs. Now the red flowers are grown in 24 provinces. In an earlier era, CIA planes carried refined white heroin from Southeast Asia to the ghettos of the US, helping quell the political and social unrest of the 1960s. It has been pointed out that although the huge majority of those imprisoned in the drug war are of the Black or Brown persuasions, there are no cocaine labs in the ghetto or barrio. However, there are meth labs a'plenty in the rural countryside, where marijuana-deprived **Angry White Folks** cook up speed by the pound; it's a wonder they don't give a ribbon for it at the county fair in some areas.

The drug war has been used as the boogey-man to justify numerous encroachments into the Constitutionally-protected rights of those suspected of or charged with drug crimes; however, when such protections are removed for one, they are lost to all.

Divinatory Meanings: Competition. Sham warfare. Struggle, labor. Search for riches and fortune. *Reversed:* Competition stifled. Trickery. Legal dispute. Mandatory minimum sentences, government seizure of properties. Busting patients at medical cannabis co-ops.

BUSHES
Four

In the foreground, four *Bushes* frame an area where two scantily-clad female dancers perform. Behind them, an arched bridge passes over a moat leading to **Offshore Banking**. There is a resemblance between this edifice and that which is destroyed on *Trump XVI*, the *Watergate,* but no symbolic connection is expressed or implied.

Divinatory Meanings: Refuge. Harvest. Repose. Romance. Peace and prosperity. New money. *Reversed:* The meaning is unaltered. *Or,* Loss of tranquility; tarnished paradise; grubby tourists in all the best places.

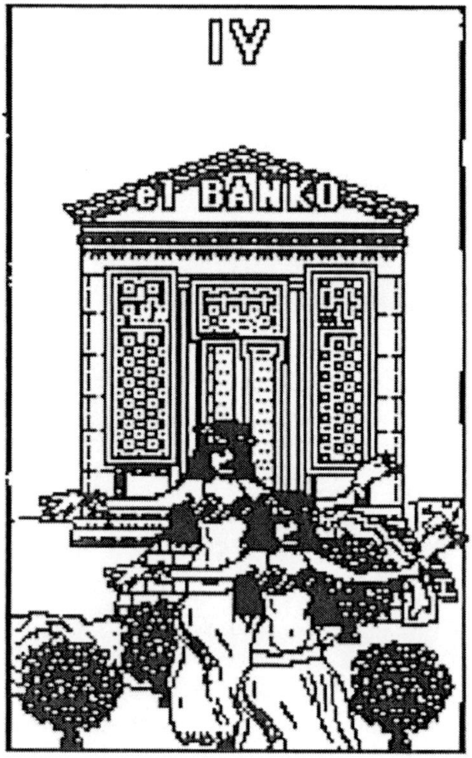
IV
el BANKO

BUSHES
Three

In the foreground, holding one *Bush* aloft and with two growing at his feet, a well-dressed man gazes out to sea. A small flotilla traverses the calm waters. This card represents **Political Action Committees**, devices by which politicians may circumnavigate prevailing currents favoring individual and corporate campaign contribution limits, and opposing the windy influence of paid lobbyists and commercial interests in government. Yet truly there is little other type of influence in that arena; just as the *Moon* governs the tides, so too does Big Business govern us all. The PAC veils and softens the raw exercise of financial clout, allowing, as it were, a number of ships to come in for the successful elected official, all registered in different ports of call, flying many flags, and carrying many cargoes; yet almost all representing the same Company in some manner.

Divinatory Meanings: Enterprise. Commerce. Discovery. Help from a successful merchant. Practical assistance. Casino-spa vacation on lobbyist's expense account. *Reversed:* The end of trouble, toil and disappointment. You want massage with happy ending? *Or,* ulterior motives. Beware of help offered! Campaign finance limits.

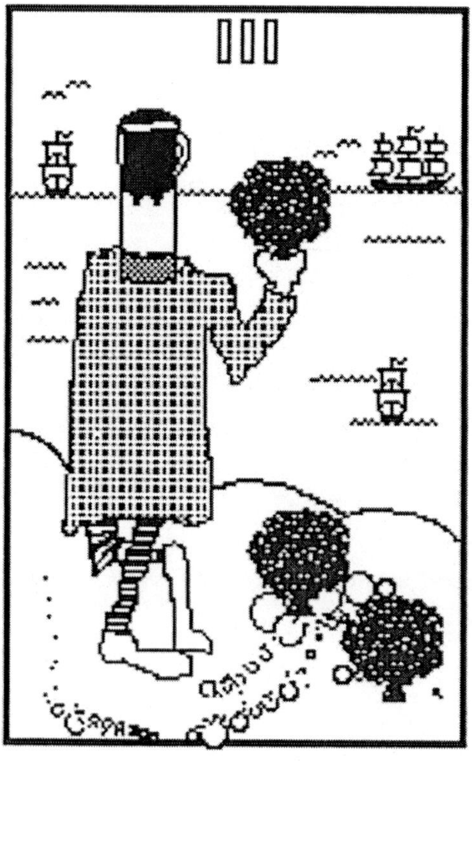

BUSHES
Two

The **Heritage Foundation**, the most widely quoted think tank in the US, is represented as a far-seeing man overlooking his domain, and holding a globe aloft. Two *Bushes* grow at his feet. We are not shown his face, in keeping with the semi-anonymous nature of foundation spokespersons. Established in 1973 with a quarter million dollar gift from Colorado anti-union brewer Joseph Coors, Heritage maintains its tax-exempt, non-profit status by claiming that it doesn't "lobby" Congress -- it just generates a top-down storm of press releases, position papers, analyses, and seminars to support whatever conservative positions need bolstering, e.g., in the early 1990s, the "intellectual underpinnings" of the Contract with America; in the early 2000s, how to regenerate that Republican "revolution" as Democrats struggle -- as usual -- to wield an unaccustomed Congressional majority. Big **Media** mouthpieces swallow this puffery whole, as it is easier than research and reporting, and spew it back to the public as "expert commentary". (The Heritage Foundation, let us say, is but the most influential of a whole passel of such policy palaces on the Potomac.)

The setting of this card recalls the mountains and terraced rice paddies of South Korea, and here's why: Heritage accepts several hundred thousand dollars annually from South Korean sources. In a report on the trial of former South Korean leaders who massacred hundreds of pro-democracy protestors there in 1980, Heritage called those murdered "rioters". The *New York Times* reported the spurious characterization, but failed to comment on the Foundation's ties to South Korea's masters.[cxxii]

Divinatory Meanings: Maturity, success, attainment. Domination, control. Autocracy. Boredom. No more worlds to conquer. *Reversed:* Surprise, wonder, enchantment, fear. Shock and awe. Unremitting greed justified by supposed intellectual superiority.

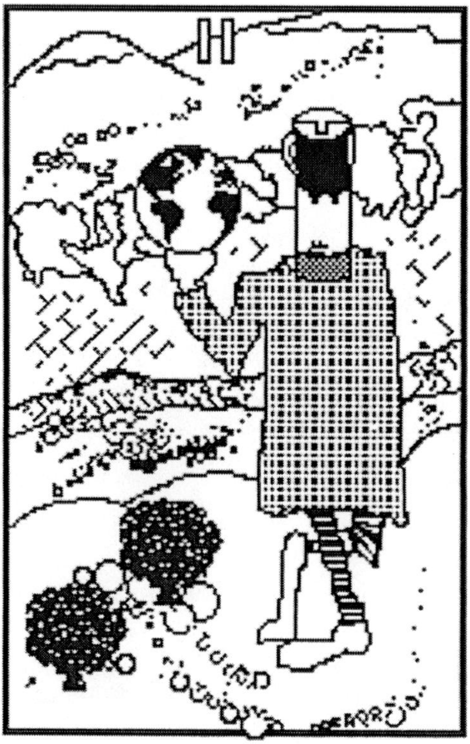

BUSHES
Ace

A hand issuing from a cloud grasps a stout green *Bush* above a sparsely treed landscape. The card represents **Paternalism**, and is called, by some, "*El Patrón*".

Divinatory Meanings: Birth, family, origins, virility. Money, inheritance, fortune, destiny. Youthful escapade. *Reversed:* Fall, decadence, ruin. Rootlessness. Cloudy outlook. Empty existence. Empire of shadows.

Ace of Bushes

Suite of Pineapples.

Pineapples
Player

Former Senator and Majority Leader **Robert Dole (R-KS)**, who proved he was a real risk-taker by resigning after thirty-five years there to seek the Republican Presidential nomination and the White House in 1996, is shown here as our Player of Pineapples. Satire is *so* unfair - his is *not* the Dole family that has fruit plantations all over the Third World; in fact this particular Dole grew up very poor; his family couldn't afford peach pits. Other unfortunate connotations of his name may, however, wield an influence over the course of affairs, and made the choice irresistible: "dole" as in "on the dole", or a career politician; "dole-" as in "doleful" or "dolorous". Robert Dole does have more spunk than the average political hack; he once said that he should be elected because, *"We've never had a President named Bob."* (A *very* arcane connection may be made here to Bob Dobbs, godhead of the Church of the Subgenius.)

Divinatory Meanings: Experienced man of business or law. Seniority. Lofty expectations. *Reversed:* Arrogance. Artistic temper. Inflexibility. Considerable loss. Reach exceeding grasp.

Player of Pineapples

Pineapples
Lady

Elizabeth Dole is the Lady of Pineapples. She is beautiful and seems dreamy, but this is only one of her faces. She sees, but she also acts, and her actions nourish her dreams. She is a former Secretary of Transportation, former Secretary of Labor, and former head of the American Red Cross, and these achievements are reflected in her gown's design. "Liddy" Dole was eminently quaified for a place on the Republican National ticket herself; did this help or hurt **Bob**'s chances?

Divinatory Meanings: Good, fair, devoted woman. Admired. Pleasure. Virtue. Nurturance. Healing. Applied intellect. *Reversed:* Not to be trusted. Exceeding accepted boundaries. Overly qualified. Uppity wimmin, castrating over-achievers.

Lady of Pineapples

Pineapples
Knave

A Republican propagandist who coined the phrase *silent majority*,[cxxiii] talking head, Presidential advisor, and three-time loser **Patrick J. Buchanan**, the Knave of Pineapples, trots across tricky territory on a bright pony. His propeller beanie seems to lift him above the terrain; or is he dreaming, a small boy on a big ride?

In 1964, as a young editor, he supported Barry Goldwater's presidential bid. He traveled with **Nixon**'s 1966 and 1968 campaigns. When Nixon was President, Buchanan was advisor and speechwriter to him and "wacky" Veep Spiro Agnew. He testified before the Senate *Watergate* committee on his role in Nixon's "Attack Group", but wasn't accused of wrongdoing. Mourning the scandal, he said: *"To effect a... counter-revolution ... there is no substitute for a principled and dedicated man of the Right in the Oval Office."* When Nixon resigned, Buchanan became an assistant to **Ford**, and later, Communications Director for **Reagan**.[cxxiv]

In 1992, Buchanan ran for President, advocating economic nationalism, reduced immigration, and social conservatism against incumbent **George H.W. Bush**, who he later supported. He spoke at the Republican Convention, describing a "culture war": *"a religious war... for the soul of America"*, attacking **Bill** and **Hillary Clinton**.[cxxv]

Buchanan again sought the Republican nod in 1996, opposing the North American Free Trade Agreement (NAFTA), following the lead of **Ross Perot**. He beat **Bob Dole** in one primary, but Dole won the rest. Buchanan threatened a third party run if Dole chose a pro-choice running mate; Dole did not.

In 2000, Buchanan was the Reform Party candidate. With the Party split between Buchanan and a gent whose platform was founded on Transcendental Meditation, founder **Ross Perot** didn't endorse either man. Dueling conventions at opposite ends of the Long Beach Convention Center nominated the two rival candidates. Finally, Buchanan won ballot status. He proposed US withdrawal from the United Nations; abolishing the Internal Revenue Service, the Departments of Education, Energy, and Housing & Urban Development;

Knave of Pineapples

taxes on inheritance and capital gains; and ending affirmative action. In one **Florida** county, he got 3,407 votes, thanks to the unwieldy "butterfly ballot". Reform Party officials estimated his actual support there at 400-500 voters.

Buchanan was an independent for a while, but before 2004, he was again a Republican, said he wouldn't run for president, and would vote for **George W. Bush**. Nevertheless, he now says the party has abandoned its conservative principles. An isolationist, he says terror groups target the US "for what we do, not who we are". He was an early, outspoken critic of the second **Iraq War**, calling Saddam Hussein more stable than American alternatives.[cxxvi]

Divinatory Meanings: A dreamer. Imagination. Arrival, approach. Invitation, proposition. Challenger. Controlling the platform. *Reversed:* Trickery, artifice, fraud, swindling. Demagoguery. Opportunism. A sly, cunning person.

Pineapples
Varlet

Log Cabin Republicans, an organization of **Gay and Lesbian** voters, got its start in the 1970s defeating a ballot initiative in California which would've kept gay people from teaching in public schools there. Former California Governor and future President **Ronald Reagan** opposed the proposal, and it was rejected.

Log Cabin works to advance the cause of equality and return the Party to its unifying principles. In 2006, Republicans lost the Congressional majority because the party alienated independent voters, who supported Democrats 57% to 39% — a sharp change from recent elections. Pollsters across the spectrum agree this made the difference in that election.

For 2008, Log Cabin says the Republican Party must offer a hopeful, *big tent* vision. "We are optimistic... because more Republicans every day understand why equality and liberty matter for every citizen, regardless of their sexual orientation. Log Cabin... stands as a principled voice working to build a more inclusive GOP and a better America."[cxxvii]

Such optimism is nothing less than inspirational among members of a Party which, according to one commentator, in the late 1970's "seized control of every branch of the U.S. government in part through vicious gay-baiting... After **Bill Clinton**'s first [Presidential] victory in 1992, Republicans immediately and relentlessly attacked him for tolerating gays in the military.

"In 2004, [**George W.**] **Bush** and the Republican Party made... opposition to gay marriage the centerpiece of their campaign. They put anti-gay marriage amendments on state ballots to turn out homophobic voters. They furiously attacked [Democratic nominee] John Kerry for pointing out... that **Dick Cheney**'s own daughter is openly gay."[cxxviii]

In this card, a fair (sunburned), rather effeminate youth contemplates a vicious crab which has jumped out of his pail to chomp his finger. It is the evil deeds of repressed Republican weirdos taking form in the news. The *Pineapples* of his suite, seen on distant trees, are far from his grasp.

Varlet of Pineapples

Divinatory Meanings: A studious young person who renders a service towards a specific goal. Reflected glamour. Meditation. Application to business. *Reversed:* Poor taste, deception. Deviation. Just because you're paranoid doesn't mean no one is talking about you behind your back!

Pineapples
Ten

Pineapples appear in a brilliant rainbow, framing a blazing sun. A group representing **Family Values** stands together on the shifting plain of standards, laws, mores, opinions, fads, urban legends and made-for-T.V. consumerism. Despite a glowing aura of peace and prosperity, they appear pensive.

Divinatory Meanings: Perfect love and friendship between a man and a woman. Contentment. *Reversed:* Indignation, violence, family quarrel. Daddy's drinking and Mommy's taking pills. Daytime television, kiddie porn on the Internet.

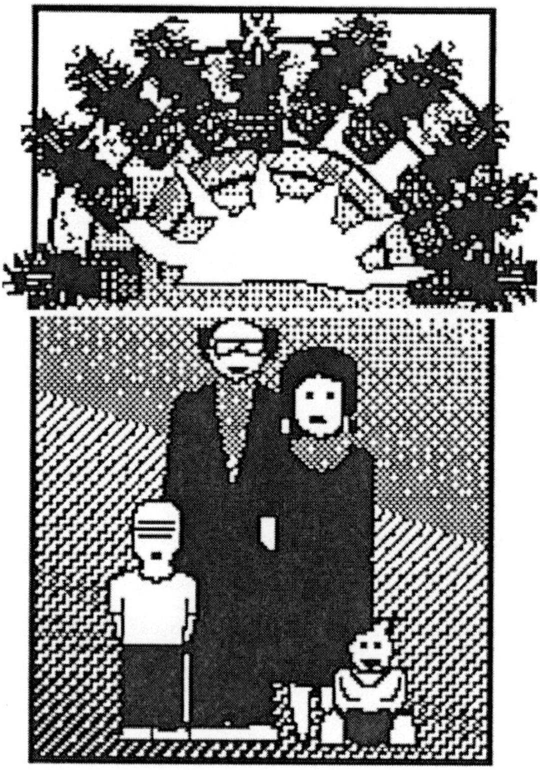

Pineapples
Nine

Conservative columnist, author and pit bull polemicist **Ann Coulter** sits surrounded by the *Pineapples* of wealth and position. Her smugness comes naturally. An "upper middle class" girl, her attorney father was a "union buster". After law school, Coulter specialized in corporate law. She worked for the US Senate Judiciary Committee after the 1994 Republican victory. She handled crime and immigration issues, helping write legislation to make it easier to deport aliens convicted of felonies.

Coulter became a public figure as an advisor in Paula Jones' sexual harassment suit against lecherous President **Bill Clinton**. Coulter's main contribution was leaking to the **Media** Clinton's "distinguishing characteristic" — a supposedly bent member that Jones could recognize and describe.

Once a starlet of conservative commentary, Coulter has lately become a kind of terrorist-age **Joseph McCarthy**, advocating a warlike response to terrorism and criticizing the Department of Transportation's refusal to use racial profiling in airport screening. When one ethnicity-driven screening attempt sparked a call for Muslims to boycott the offending airline, Coulter said, "*If only we could get Muslims to boycott all airlines, we could dispense with airport security altogether.*" Here are some of her other shock-jock-worthy remarks:

"[Clinton] masturbates in the [White House] sinks." — *Rivera Live* 8/2/99

"{Humans] have dominion over... plants... animals... trees. God said, '*Earth is yours. Take it. Rape it. It's yours.*'" — *Hannity & Colmes*, 6/20/01

The "backbone of the Democratic Party" is a "fat... welfare recipient" — syndicated column, 10/29/99

To a disabled Vietnam vet: "People like you caused us to lose that war." — MSNBC

"I think there should be a literacy test and a poll tax for people to vote." — *Hannity & Colmes*, 8/17/99

"I think [women] should be armed but should not [be allowed to] vote." — *Politically Incorrect*, 2/26/01

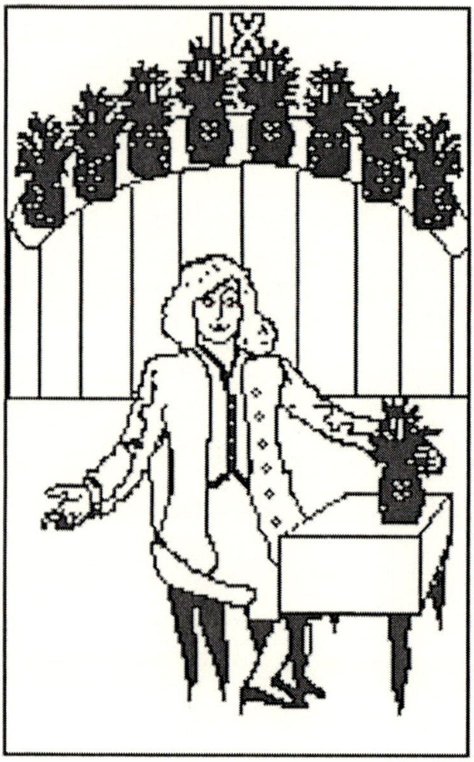
IX

"I am emboldened by my looks to say things Republican men wouldn't."
— *TV Guide* 8/97[cxxix]

At this writing Coulter is under fire for saying, "*I was going to... comment... on... Democratic presidential candidate John Edwards but... you have to go into rehab if you use the word 'faggot,' so... I'll just conclude...*"[cxxx]

Divinatory Meanings: Abundance. An assured future. Well-being. Complacency. Advantages. Blondes have more fun. *Reversed:* Mistakes. Imperfections. Misplaced truth. False freedom. Miscalculation. The ancient Greeks called it *hubris*.

Pineapples
Eight

A card which is quite simple to understand, when the Big Picture is seen, and How Things Really Work is understood. The *Eight of Pineapples* is represented here as Congressional commitment to the concept of **Term Limits**, by which it is hoped that New Blood and New Brooms will be elected regularly by the simple expedient of preventing old brooms from sticking around forever. Unfortunately, the concept neglects both the tenaciousness of the incumbent, and the fact that every election cycle is an opportunity to limit an unsatisfactory representative's term.

Divinatory Meanings: Desertion of past joys, concerns, enterprises. Gettin' on down the road. "Put it on the agenda next term." A matter which has been thought important is of small consequence, once you get into office yourself. Shyness, modesty. *Reversed:* Great joy. A feast; an election fundraiser with open bar.

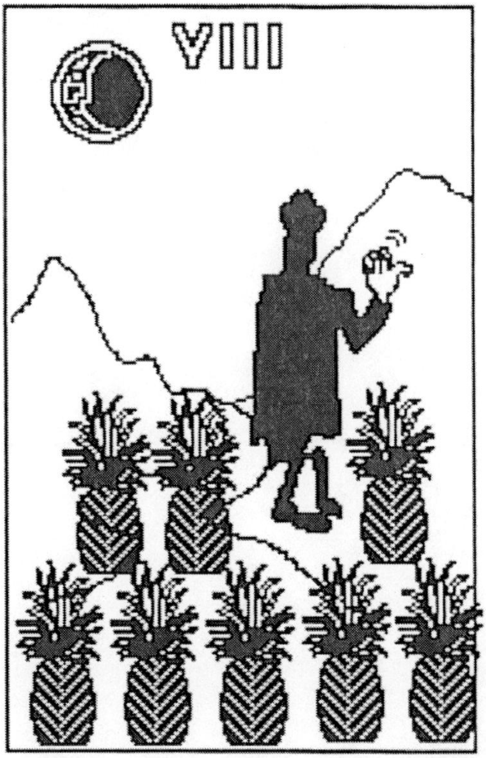
VIII

Pineapples
Seven

Pineapples filled with Republican dreams -- wealth, power, industrial deregulation, strip mining national forests, mandatory school prayer and "intelligent design", reverse affirmative action, etc. -- float in a cloud, representing the **Resolutions Committee** of the National Republican Convention. These resolutions may appear unreal, and at the time of writing, some of them are. Yet it is from today's dreams that tomorrow's platform will come, and who is to say what cannot be achieved? The committee member in the foreground has one hand on her head; perhaps in amazement at what is offered for her consideration and approval; perhaps nursing a severe hangover.

Divinatory Meanings: Fantasy, daydreams, whims. Wishful thinking. Illusions. Imaginary honors. Nothing permanent is gained. *Reversed:* Desire, will, determination. A goal nearly attained. Resolutions. Four -- or forty -- more years!

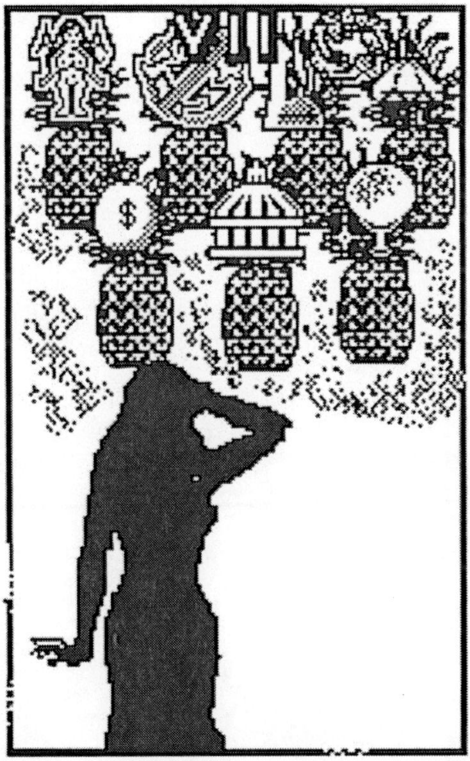

Pineapples
Six

Late US Rep. **Sonny Bono** (**R-CA**, 1994-98) and his former protegé and ex-wife, singer/actress **Cher**, appear as **Innocent Youth** here, examining the *Pineapples* in an old California garden.

Salvatore "Sonny" Bono was born in 1935 in Detroit. When he was 7, his family moved to California, but Sonny was able to find them. Sonny wrote songs in his spare time. He tried a solo singing career, but didn't do well. Selling songs to Sunset Boulevard labels in the late 50's, he got a job with producer Phil Spector. In 1964, The Searchers recorded his *Needles and Pins*. About this time, he met Cherilyn Sarkisian, a 16-year old club singer. Sonny left his first wife and married Cher. A few months later, they recorded *I Got You Babe*. In 1965, they had five songs in the Billboard Top 100, an achievement then matched only by the Beatles. By late 1967, Sonny and Cher had sold 40 million records.

As the 60s waned, they developed a nightclub act. In 1971, they starred in CBS's *Sonny & Cher Comedy Hour*. The show, written mostly by Sonny, played him as a buffoon against Cher's smart aleck persona. The couple split in 1974.

Bono opened a restaurant in Palm Springs. Hassled by city zoning officials, he took on city hall. He won that battle, then ran for Mayor and won. Sonny didn't register to vote until age 52, but was a natural politician.

He was elected to Congress in 1994, and re-elected in 1996, one of just two non-lawyers on the Judiciary Committee. He supported the conservative Republican agenda and became the focus of many late night television jokes. Killed when he kissed a moving tree in a skiing accident in 1998, he was succeeded in Congress by fourth wife Mary .

Briefly wedding Southern rocker Greg Allman, Cher co-starred in *Silkwood* with Meryl Streep and won an Oscar. In 1987 she had three hit films. In the 90s, she again became a rock-pop star. In March 1999 she ruled the Top 40, holding the No. 1 spot for four consecutive weeks, the oldest woman at that time to hit the top spot, and with the longest span

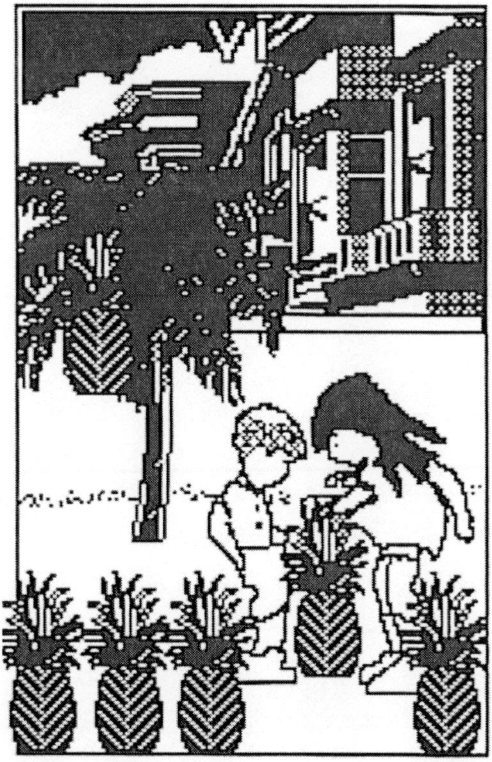

between Billboard chart toppers ('65-'99) of any pop recording artist.[cxxxi]

When Sonny and Cher's daughter, Chastity, came out as a lesbian and began working for **Gay** rights, Cher, who had little previous interest in politics, supported her. She has since been active in many liberal and progressive causes, including the peace movement.[cxxxii]

Divinatory Meanings: The past, i.e., the Sixties. "I got you, babe!" *Reversed:* The future. Renewal. Plans that may fail. Male pattern baldness.

Pineapples
Five

The 44th Vice President, **Dan Quayle** (1989-1993), stands by a window, three prone *Pineapples* on the floor before him. Two others, upright, are behind him, but he may not see them. Outside, a broken bridge leads to the White House. He has been awaiting a call for some time.

In 1976, Quayle was elected to Congress (**R-IN**), defeating an 8-term incumbent Democrat. He was re-elected in 1978 by the greatest percentage margin achieved to that date in his district. In 1980, at 33, he became the youngest person ever sent to the Senate from Indiana, defeating a 3-term incumbent Democrat. He was re-elected in 1986 with the largest numerical margin to that date in a statewide Indiana race. Quayle sat on the Armed Services, Budget, and Labor and Human Resources Committees. In 1988, **George H. W. Bush** tapped him as his running mate, and the duo won, despite questions about Quayle's use of family connections to get into the National Guard and avoid possible combat in Vietnam.

As Vice President, Quayle was revealed as a ninny. He received the satirical "Ig Nobel Prize" for "demonstrating... the need for science education" in 1991. Critics said he was a good reason for Bush critics to pray for Bush's health, and the only Veep to make his President "impeachment-proof"; this, of course, preceded **Dick Cheney**'s term!

Quayle's provided much grist for comics' mills. ("*The future will be better tomorrow*"; "*For NASA, space is still a high priority*"; and "*It's time for the human race to enter the solar system*" are memorable). As Veep, Quayle chaired the National Space Council. Asked about sending humans to Mars, he said, "*Mars is essentially in the same orbit [as Earth].... [and] somewhat the same distance from the Sun, which is very important. We have seen pictures where there are canals, we believe, and water. If there is water... there is oxygen. If oxygen... we can breathe.*"

He criticized gangsta rap and denounced Tupac Shakur's debut album as having "*no place in our society*." At the Commonwealth Club of California, Quayle blamed the Rodney King riots on decaying **Family Values** and a fictional character in a television program, *Murphy Brown*.

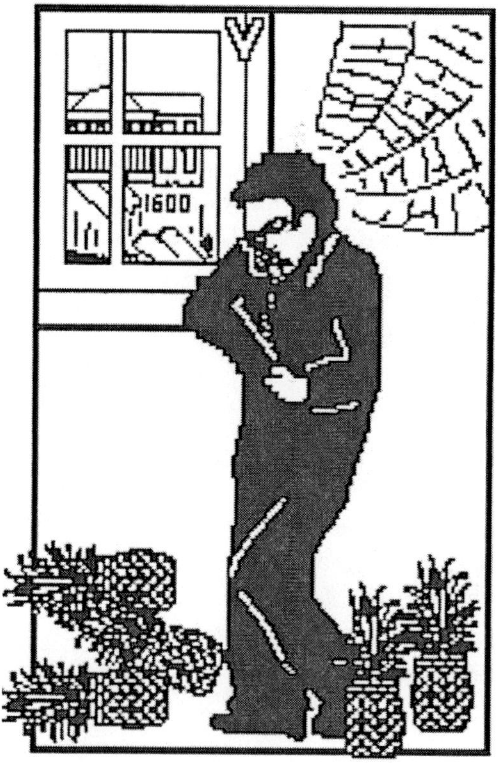
V
1600

"It doesn't help matters when primetime TV has Murphy Brown — a character who supposedly epitomizes today's intelligent, highly paid, professional woman — mocking the importance of fathers, by bearing a child alone, and calling it just another 'lifestyle choice.'" The remark drew a firestorm of ridicule and criticism and became one of the most memorable incidents of the dull 1992 Presidential race. Even after the brouhaha ended, the comment echoed in US politics for years, in kneejerk outcries against the collapse of the family.

Bush I and Quayle lost their '92 re-election bid. Quayle pulled out of the 1996 Republican race, citing health problems. He tried again in 2000, attacking **George W. Bush** by saying, *"we do not want another candidate who needs on-the-job training"*; however, this merely reminded voters of his own on-the-job performance. In the first contest among Republican candidates, in Iowa, he finished eighth, and took the hint. Commentators said that, while he had more experience than Bush II or **Elizabeth Dole**, and grassroots support among some conservatives, he was hampered by his own vice-presidency.[cxxxiii]

Quayle's ambitions might best have been summed up in this quote: *"People that are really very weird can get into sensitive positions and have a tremendous impact on history."*

Divinatory Meanings: Partial loss. Inheritance, but not as expected. Imperfection. Meaningless friendships. The Vice Presidency. Keepin' it weird. *Reversed:* News, alliances, affinity. Return of an old friend: Mr. Potatoe Head.

Pineapples
Four

Warren G. Harding, 29th President (1921-1923) and sixth to die in office, was a publisher with a flair for public speaking. He served in the Ohio Senate, was Lieutenant Governor of Ohio, and was a US Senator from 1915 until his inauguration, the first sitting Senator elected President.

Harding was a "dark horse", winning the Republican nod at a deadlocked convention where kingmakers met in a smoke-filled room. Harding, when asked if there was anything in his past that might be used against him (his education was limited, he was a drinker just as **Alcohol Prohibition** was coming into existence, and he'd been accused of having **Sex** with his Senate press secretary), just said, "*No*", and was selected. The Party learned soon enough of his longtime affair with Carrie Fulton Phillips, wife of an old friend. Phillips and her family took a slow boat to China, courtesy of the Party, in return for her silence. She received monthly payments thereafter, the only person publicly known to have successfully extorted a major political party.

Harding's "front porch campaign" was the first to be heavily covered by press and newsreels, and to use the power of Hollywood and Broadway stars, who traveled to Marion, OH, for photo opportunities with Harding and his wife. Al Jolson, Lillian Russell, Douglas Fairbanks and Mary Pickford, as well as businessmen Thomas Edison, Henry Ford, and Harvey Firestone visited Harding. His support for women's suffrage in the Senate made him popular with **Women**. He won in a landslide.

Due to the scandals in his administration, Harding is often rated the worst President ever. He himself said, "*I am not fit for this office and never should have been here.*" In the Teapot Dome affair, his Interior Secretary, Albert B. Fall, took bribes in exchange for leasing public oil fields to pals. Fall was the first ever Cabinet member to go to prison, but not the last! The director of the Veterans Bureau skimmed profits, took kickbacks, and led illegal alcohol and drug distribution networks. No one suggests that Harding profited from these crimes, but he couldn't stop them. "*My G-d, this is a hell of a job!*" he said. "*I have no trouble with my enemies, but... my G-d-damned friends... keep me walking the floor nights!*"

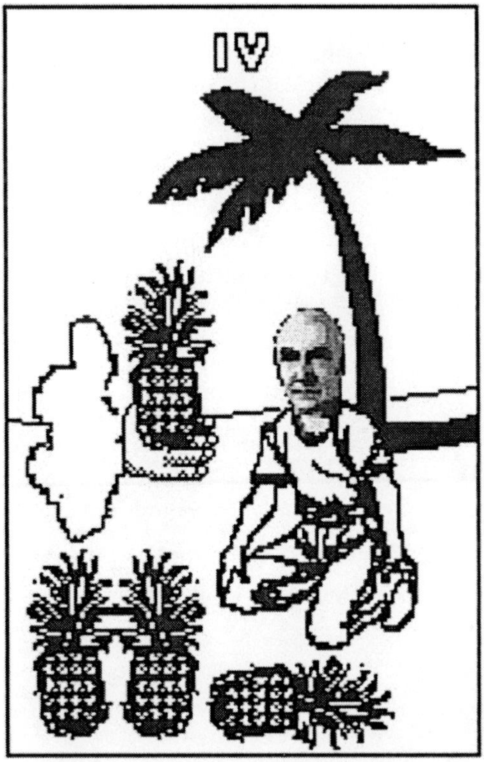
IV

Besides Carrie Phillips, Harding carried on with Nan Britton, the daughter of another crony. She wrote that she and Harding conceived a child in his Senate office, who Harding never met but supported. Some say they continued their affair while he was President, in a closet near the Oval Office, later re-dedicated to that purpose by Mr. **Clinton**.

Although a noted speaker, Harding had frequent verbal lapses, compounded by his writing his own speeches. H.L. Mencken said, "*He writes the worst English that I have ever encountered. It reminds me of... wet sponges... tattered washing on the line... stale bean soup, of college yells, of dogs barking idiotically through endless nights. It is so bad that a sort of grandeur creeps into it.*" Upon Harding's death, poet E.E. Cummings said, "*The only man... who wrote a simple declarative sentence with seven grammatical errors is dead.*"[cxxxiv]

In our *IV of Pineapples*, a white-haired man sits by a palm tree, with a pensive look. In front of him, a hand issuing from a cloud, reminiscent of the one appearing on the *Ace* of this suite, offers him a *Pineapple*. Three other *Pineapples* rest on the ground nearby; one is overturned. He shows no interest in them. The setting could be a desert island, and it is this which brings to mind the sociable Harding's delimma in the years of enforced thirst he endured as a Prohibition President, and the poignant lament of Coleridge's Ancient Mariner: "*Water, water everywhere, but not a drop to drink!*" Then again, he may be thinking of other loves, and the well-known maxim, "*Candy is dandy, but liquor is quicker!*"

Divinatory Meanings: Weariness, discontent, aversion. Virgin martinis. No consolation in material gain. *Reversed:* Novelty, new relations. An old friend's daughter.

Pineapples
Three

The end of **Alcohol Prohibition** is depicted as the *III of Pineapples*. Mrs. Pauline Morton Sabin, Mrs. Grace Root and Mrs. William Lowell Putnam, somewhat fancifully, dance with abandon among the *Pineapples* of their suite; they were among the most prominent **Republican Women** who, in 1929, formed the Women's Organization for National Prohibition Reform to oppose the Women's Christian Temperance Union, thus making it possible, after nine years of Prohibition, for "respectable" politicians to publicly oppose it. Contributing substantively to repeal of the 18th Amendment, members of WONPR were vilified as "wine drinkers" and "social cocktail drinkers"; many did not drink, but opposed the widespread criminality and warped law enforcement priorities Prohibition bred.[cxxxv] However, little umbrellas in these *Pineapples* suggest that they may contain tropical drinks; also, is that a breast, or is the gentle lady in the forefront holding a globe of some other type aloft? *Things are not always as they seem.*

Divinatory Meanings: A happy ending. Healing, mending. *Reversed:* Excess physical enjoyment and fleshly pleasures. Superfluity, overabundance. Rich and spoiled. Girls gone wild!

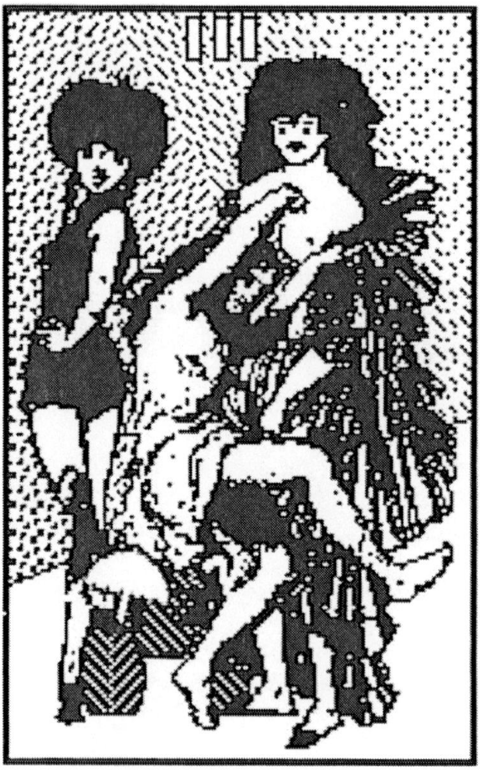
III

Pineapples
Two

Alluding to the infamous **Hayes-Tilden Compromise of 1877**, defeated Democrat Samuel J. "Tweedledum" **Tilden** and Republican President-elect Rutherford B. "Tweedledee" **Hayes** pledge agreement that federal troops will be withdrawn from the South, and Reconstruction ended; in return for Hayes' Congressional selection as the 19th President, and the Southern states' agreement not to secede again. From their raised *Pineapples*, two hooded cobras rise, representing racism in the North and in the South. Cross burnings by the Ku Klux Klan darken the atmosphere.

Divinatory Meanings: Love, friendship, Union, sympathy, the interrelation of opposites. Passion. Cooperation, mutual satisfaction. *Reversed:* The meaning is not altered. *Or*, unsatisfactory love, troubled relationship, divorce, secession. *Also,* haggle, horse-trade, quibble, squabble, wrangle, wrassle. Sell-out; hostile take-over. Deal with the *Devil. Or,* Deliverance.

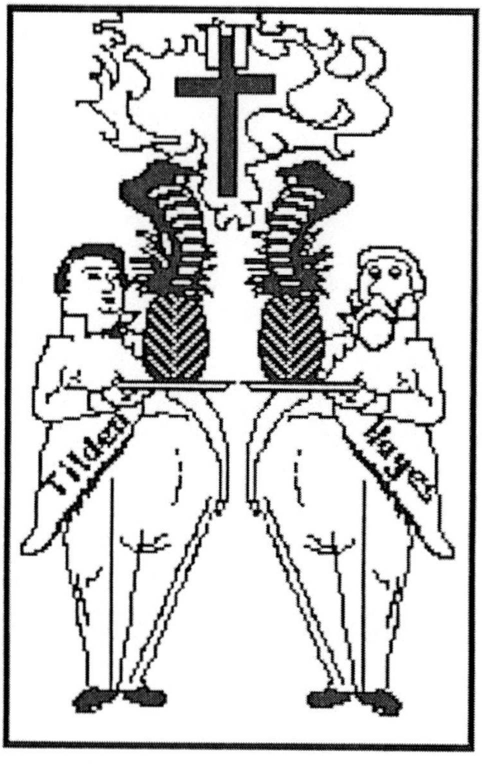

Tilden
Hayes

Pineapples
Ace

The bountiful Hawaiian Islands, now the 51st State, once a peaceful, independent monarchy, lie below a cloud-borne hand in this *very* traditional interpretation. The card quite simply denotes **Imperialism**. Note that the hand holds a ripe *Pineapple*, but we call those client states, which have not been absorbed into the Union, "Banana Republics". Four fountains of Juice spurt from the rich fruit, one in each of the cardinal directions. A fish leaps in a rising, warming sea.

Some Pacific Islands have already disappeared, and others worldwide may have to be abandoned if melting polar icecaps continue to fuel that tidal rise, reminiscent of untenable positions of privilege in a world of rising expectations.

Divinatory Meanings: Joy, contentment. Wealth, abundance. Dominion. Sexuality; fertility. *Reversed:* Unexpected loss. Hurricane season. Erosion. Sterility. Mutation, instability, revolution.

Ace of Pineapples

Suite of Arms.

ARMS
Player

Retired General and former Secretary of State (2001-2005) **Colin Powell** appears as the Player of Arms. With stern face and military demeanor, he holds an automatic weapon, the sign of his suite, aloft.

At 49, Powell, a decorated Vietnam veteran, became **Ronald Reagan**'s National Security Advisor (1987-1989). After his NSC tenure, he was promoted to four-star General by **George H.W. Bush**, joining **Eisenhower** and Alexander Haig as the only men to reach that rank since World War II without having been divisional commanders. His last posting was as Chairman of the Joint Chiefs of Staff (1989-1995), the highest military position in the Department of Defense. At 52, he was the youngest to have this job, the first Jamaican-American, and the first Reserve Officers Training Corps (ROTC) graduate. He oversaw 28 military crises and operations, including the US invasion of Panama to remove General Manuel Noriega from power.[cxxxvi] Called "the reluctant warrior", Powell rarely advocated military interventions, preferring diplomacy and containment

In 1990, Powell opposed deploying troops to force Iraqi leader Saddam Hussein out of neighboring Kuwait, believing the dictator could be contained through sanctions and strengthened forces around him.[cxxxvii] But when the decision to invade was taken, Powell efficiently directed the US-led, UN-sanctioned "Operation Desert Storm" (a.k.a., First **Iraq War**.)

After retiring, popular and respected, he was considered as a possible Presidential candidate, but preferred to campaign for others. In Texas, he backed **George W. Bush** for Governor.

Powell's "meteoric rise through a system that operated in an essentially rational way"[cxxxviii] -- the Army -- ill-prepared him for his later term as Secretary of State, as the Second President **Bush**'s increasingly wacky policies played out before an increasingly unamused world. Following attacks on the US on Sept. 11, 2001, Powell urged caution, opposing Bush's desire to attack the resurgent Hussein; but he was "used, mastered, and... cast aside... [by] longtime colleague **Dick Cheney**."[cxxxix]

Player of Arms

Powell has himself said that he will be most remembered for his pivotal, dramatic speech to the UN Security Council in 2003, vouching for the existence of "weapons of mass destruction" in Iraq -- an assertion later revealed to be almost totally false, and known then to be false by Powell's assistants, suborned by pro-war partisans.

Divinatory Meanings: Intellectual force. Power of life or death. Commander. A professional man. Highly analytical. Military intelligence is to intelligence as military music is to music. Sitting in judgment. *Reversed:* Someone who may pursue a matter too far. Aggression, cruelty. *Or,* disdain for the fray; a sword unblooded. Tactical success at the price of strategic failure.

ARMS
Lady

Secretary of State **Condoleezza Rice** (2005 – present), the first African-American woman in that office, also was first to combine her gender and race as National Security Advisor, where she was nicknamed the "Warrior Princess," for her strong nerve and delicate manner. A brilliant professor of political science at Stanford, Rice made her reputation as an analyst of the Soviet Union and Eastern Europe. In 1986, an international affairs fellow at the Council on Foreign Relations, she served in **George H.W. Bush**'s administration as Special Assistant to the Director of the Joint Chiefs of Staff, and later as Soviet and East European Affairs Advisor (1989-1991).

"Condi" as she is dimunitively known, has been ranked the most powerful woman in the world by *Forbes* (2004, 2005) and second most powerful in 2006 (after German Chancellor Angela "Angi" Merkel). She is one of only three people ranked among the world's most influential by *Time* magazine more than three times (2004, 2005, 2006, 2007).

Rice was born in Birmingham, Alabama, only child of a minister and his wife. When the civil rights movement rocked the city in the 1960s, her father stood guard as Condi practiced the piano. Rev. Rice thought local civil rights leaders "uneducated, misguided Negroes." He taught that Black people must prove themselves worthy of advancement, and be "twice as good" as Whites, to overcome racism.

Growing up under segregation taught Condi determination, and the value of the right to bear *Arms*, the sign of her suite. She has said that if gun registration had been mandatory, her father's weapons would have been confiscated, leaving them defenseless against the Ku Klux Klan.

Rice first joined the State Department in 1977, in the Democratic Carter administration. She remained a Democrat until 1982, when she switched due to Carter's hapless foreign policy. Her father had become a Republican years before when turnd away by a racist Democratic voter registrar. As she told the 2000 Republican National Convention, "*My father joined our party because the Democrats in Jim Crow Alabama of 1952 would not register him to vote. The Republicans did.*"

Lady of Arms

Rice supports Bush II's 2003 -- present **Iraq War**. In the 2004 Presidential race, she became the first National Security Advisor to campaign for a sitting President. She said, "*Saddam Hussein had nothing to do with the* [Sept. 11, 2001] *attacks on America,* [but his] *Iraq was a part of the Middle East that was festering and unstable,* [and] *was part of the circumstances that created the problem.*" Indeed, as contradictions between Dubya's foreign policy and the rest of the world become increasingly sharp, the inscrutable Rice has immersed herself more and more in the perpetual desert of the Middle East, in particular the Israeli-Palestinian fraternal conflict, where shifting sands of allegiance and betrayal mock the most brilliant negotiators.

When Rice became Secretary of State, after **Colin Powell**, she was confirmed by a Senate vote of 85-13, the most 'nays' against a nominee for that post since 1825. Sometimes called "black by accident", Condi golfs, is an accomplished pianist (plays Brahms; digs Led Zeppelin and Cream); her fave flix are *Casablanca* and *The Way We Were*. We think *Lawrence of Arabia* is also in her Top 10! Dream job? National Football League Commissioner. Dream man? Not for this Lady; or, he remains in her dreams – *has she met* **James Meredith**?[cxl]

Divinatory Meanings: Quick witted, keen, lean and mean. Reserved, private. Unimpressed by opulence. Daddy's girl; tomboy, jockette. *Reversed:* Bigotry. Possible sadness. Loneliness. Loss. Abnegation; anorexia, amenorrhea. Amnesia, *OR*, recovered memories.

ARMS
Knave

Supreme Court Justice **Clarence Thomas** is the second African American on the high court. His grandfather taught him to "never let the sun catch you in bed." Thomas hasn't been caught in bed yet, but it may be just a matter of time! He was strongly influenced by Ayn Rand's *The Fountainhead*, in which the protagonist's struggle against conformity mirrored Thomas' career as a federal bureaucrat, at least in his mind. He began his rise with the **Reagan** administration, eventually heading the Office of Civil Rights in the Department of Education (DOE), and the Equal Employment Opportunity Commission (EEOC). In 1990, **George H.W. Bush** appointed him to the federal appeals bench.

While his later Supreme Court appointment preserved the court's racial balance, it tipped its ideological scale to the right. The NAACP, Urban League and National Organization for Women opposed his appointment based on Thomas's scorn for affirmative action and suspicion that he opposed **Roe *v.* Wade**. During his confirmation hearings, it was learned that a former colleague at DOE and EEOC, Anita Hill, had accused him of sexual harassment, but there was insufficient evidence for her claim. Testimony from another former EEOC staffer who had seen the alleged offensive conduct was suppressed. Democrats in control of the Senate were reluctant to call this witness, who Thomas had fired for calling yet *another* employee a *"faggot"*. The hearings had been quite salty already, with queries about whether Thomas had called himself *"Long Dong Silver"*, or told Ms. Hill, *"There's a pubic hair in my Coke"*.

After joining the Supreme Court, Thomas, a Catholic, obtained a Church annulment of his first marriage. In 1994, he officiated, at his home, at conservative radio host **Rush Limbaugh**'s third wedding ceremony.[cxli]

The Knave of Arms rides a dark horse, at a gallop, at dawn, from a desert height or rocky fortress, his weapon extended as he charges.

Divinatory Meanings: Skill. Dash. Nerve. Brass balls. Gallantry, chivalry, compliments. *Reversed:* Enmity, anger. Effrontery, rudeness. Recklessness. Extravagance. Dispute or ruin over a woman. Impulsive mistakes. Conceited fool.

Knave of Arms

ARMS
Varlet

Senator Joseph R. McCarthy (**R-WI**, 1947 -- 1957) authored so many odious, divisive and fear-inducing words and actions as to beggar the imagination; indeed many were beggared when they appeared on his blacklists of questioned loyalty. After World War II, loyalty was the most valued characteristic of US citizens, and blackmail a popular blood sport.[cxlii] McCarthy's paranoid witch-hunt was inspired by the Cold War. He claimed hundreds of Communists, Soviet spies and sympathizers were in the federal government. "*McCarthyism*", a term describing his methods, includes demagogic, reckless accusations, and attacks on the character or patriotism of opponents. He never substantiated his charges.

Some opposed him early. Senator Margaret Chase Smith (**R-ME**) in 1950 called for an end to "smear tactics", without actually naming McCarthy. Six other Republican Senators stood with her. McCarthy called them "*Snow White and the six dwarves.*" Ralph E. Flanders (**R-VT**) compared McCarthy to Hitler on the Senate floor, and said, "*Were the Junior Senator from Wisconsin in the pay of the Communists he could not have done a better job for them.*"

In 1952, **Eisenhower** became the first Republican President in 20 years, also holding a majority in Congress. "Ike" didn't like McCarthy and tried to reduce his power. But he never confronted him or criticized him directly, perhaps prolonging McCarthy's power, since even the President wouldn't tackle him. The Army-McCarthy hearings of 1954, broadcast on television, and McCarthy's absurd "revelations" of reds in the military, ended his influence. The Senate censured him, one of the few times a Senator has been so disciplined He died at 48 of hepatitis due to alcoholism.[cxliii]

Recently there have been attempts to rehabilitate McCarthy's image, e.g., by **Ann Coulter**. Today's "War on Terror" shares much with McCarthy's anti-Communist heyday. If "History proves" McCarthy's probity and wisdom, then History, Gentle Reader, may not be drinking enough!

Divinatory Meanings: Vigilance, alertness; awareness, insomnia. *Reversed:* Paranoia. Threat levels Red Scare, Jack Black, and John Walker Blue.

Varlet of Arms

ARMS
Ten

Ten automatic weapons pin a dark, turbaned man to the ground in a representation of what History may yet call the **Iraq Wars**. Oil fires still rage out of control in neighboring Kuwait, spewing pollution into the upper atmosphere. Like so many US wars, the first Iraq adventure began only after irresistible provocation from nutty dictator Saddam Hussein, who got his start from the US. (See *Player of Bushes*.) Late in 1996, the Department of Defense finally admitted that US troops had experienced heavy exposure to toxic chemicals during action in the First Iraq War, causing neurological, reproductive, and other health problems for many. In 2007, more than 16 years after the first war ended, one in four Gulf War veterans remained seriously ill with various medical problems. According to the chairman of a House research advisory committee, the Defense Department and Veterans Administration remained in "virtual denial" about Gulf War Veterans Illness, not even requesting continuation funding to study the complex syndrome.[cxliv]

Despite a less-than-conclusive victory in this episode, and with little or no evidence for its necessity, a second war with Iraq was launched by **George W. Bush** after Sept. 11, 2001 terrorist attacks on US soil. This time, Iraqi troops encountered were more dedicated, even after Hussein was captured and hung, and US casualties continued to mount in a destabilized, quagmire-style snafu. The name of one game in the Middle East is Oil; another is *Jihad*. The *Bush* family's longtime links to the oily Saudi Arabian ruling family, embarrassing enough in themselves, became even more embarrassing when it was revealed that these ties extended to the family of 9-Eleven's master terrorist, Osama bin Laden, but none of them seemed to realize the embarrassment.

Divinatory Meanings: Pain, affliction, trouble. Refugees. Torturing POWs. Collateral damage. Deniable post-war syndromes. Tears. *Reversed:* Profit, success, regional prestige, curried favor (but none of these are permanent).

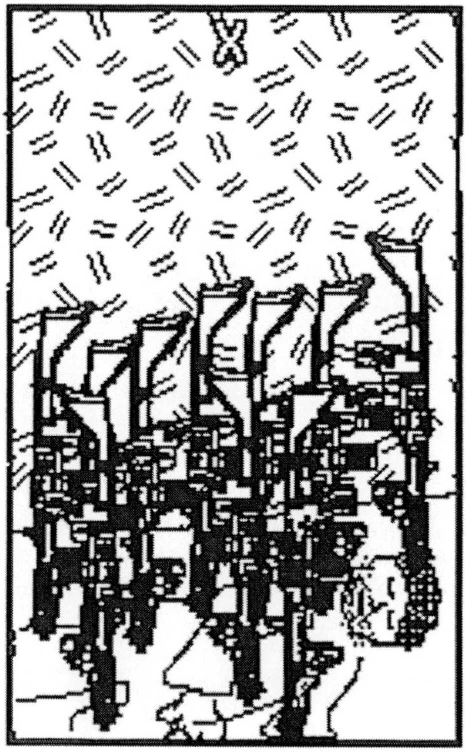

ARMS
Nine

Tammy Faye Bakker Messner (1942-2007), although not identified primarily with the Republican Party, was the tear-streaked face of the resurgent **Christian Right** (*VI of Bushes*), founding a televangelism empire with her husband, James Bakker. The couple "worked as traveling evangelists in the early years of their marriage. He preached; she sang and played the accordion. They began their television career in the mid-1960s, joining Pat Robertson's fledgling Christian Broadcasting Network as... hosts of 'The 700 Club.'

"In 1974, the Bakkers founded the Praise the Lord [PTL] network... and achieved wide popularity as hosts of the syndicated 'Jim and Tammy Show.' At its peak, in the '80s... PTL... reached as many as 13 million households, always to a drumbeat of appeals for donations.

"The Bakkers' enterprises, including Heritage USA, a 2,300-acre religious theme park and resort in Fort Mill, S.C., grew in value to more than $125 million.

"Ms. Messner... was known for appearing on camera in overstated outfits and heavy makeup. She was openly emotional, whether praying for the health of an ailing viewer or for... contributions. When she broke down on camera — and she did so often — her tears and mascara... ran copiously..."[cxlv]

In the late 1980s, the PTL empire collapsed when it was revealed that Jim had a **Sex**ual encounter with a church secretary, who was paid over $230,000 to keep quiet about it; that PTL had cheated investors in a planned hotel at the Heritage complex; and that the Bakkers lived in absurd luxury, enjoying gold-plated bath fixtures and an air conditioned doghouse. Jim Bakker was convicted of 24 fraud and conspiracy counts and spent five years of a 45-year sentence in prison.

While Jim was away, Tammy divorced him and married Roe Messner, one of the Bakkers' business associates. Two years later, in 1995, Hubby #2 was convicted of bankruptcy fraud and *he* went to prison – but Hubby #1 had been freed in 1994. Life goes on...

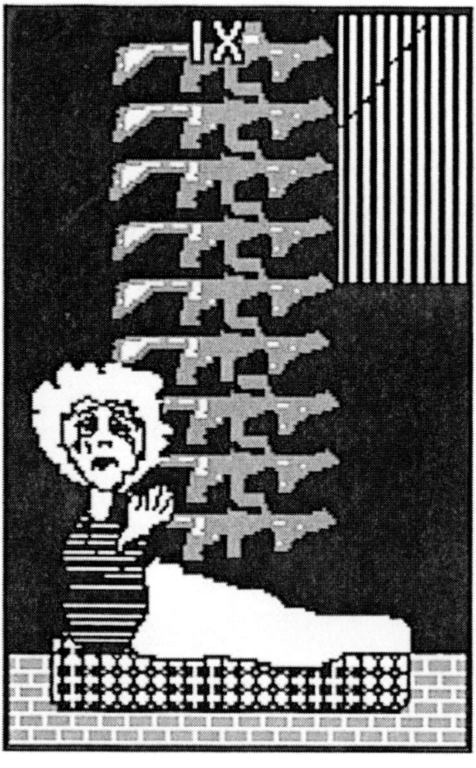
IX

"[Tammy's] troubles with drug dependency and depression made her a target of tabloid headlines.

"**Gay** men came to embrace Ms. Messner as a camp figure... She embraced them... She began attending gay pride events, and in 1996, she became the co-host of a syndicated television talk show with Jim J. Bullock, an openly gay actor."[cxlvi]

The Bakkers' son, Jay, after some youthful rebellion involving drugs, tattoos, and punk rock, followed in his parents' footsteps and started his own "Revolution Church".

"Through it all, [Mrs.] Messner kept plugging her faith and herself. She did concerts... and an inspirational video. In 2004, she cooperated in the making of a documentary about her struggle with [incurable colon] cancer called *Tammy Faye: Death Defying*."[cxlvii]

Tears and thickly-smeared makeup notwithstanding, it is Tammy Faye's imperturbability under duress which suits her for her role here; surely, she had "put on the whole armor of God", and the weeping lady of the *IX of Arms* needs divine assistance! Nine *Arms* hang suspended above her in the dark; how long can they defy gravity?

"Just recently, [Mrs. Messner's] story became the stuff of musical theater. *Big Tent: The Tammy Faye Bakker Musical*, an Off Broadway production, had its first public viewing... on May 23 at New World Stages in Manhattan."[cxlviii]

Divinatory Meanings: A quarrel. Disappointment. Anxiety over a loved one. Worry. Miscarriage of justice. *Reversed:* Imprisonment, suspicion, reasonable doubt, shame.

ARMS
Eight

A bound and blindfolded woman, representing the perenially-threatened **Roe** *v.* **Wade** decision of 1970, which allows women in the US to have legal abortions, stands surrounded by eight *Arms*. The exercise of so-called "pro-life" activism has led to women's health clinics being similarly beset: bombed; doctors threatened, and even murdered, for performing abortions; and women needing police protection when seeking abortions, or even information about birth control. Federal court appointments have hinged upon jurist's perceived or recorded views on the subject. However, like the condition of pregnancy itself, this is a card of temporary, rather than permanent, bondage.

Divinatory Meanings: Division. Crisis. Calamity. Bad news. Criticism. Sickness, weakness. A fatality. Baby-killers! *Reversed:* Disquiet, opposition, treachery. Suspicious packages; abandoned babies. Return of the back-alley abortionist. The unforeseen. "*Your daughter is pregnant, Mrs. Schafley.*"[cxlix]

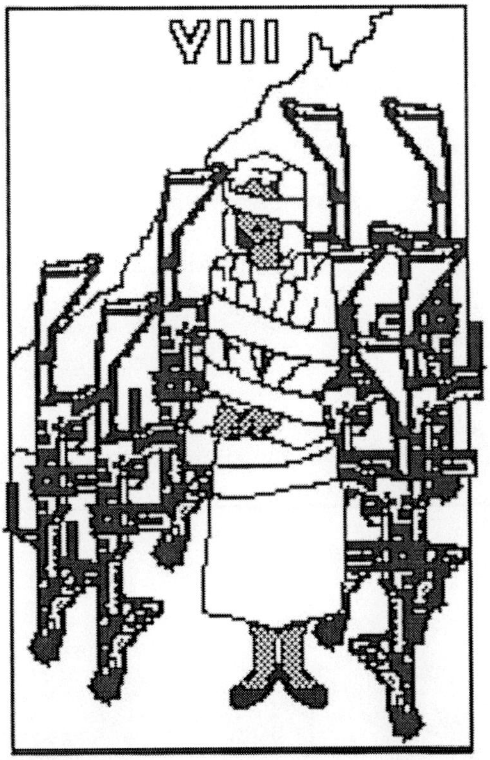
VIII

ARMS
Seven

A man representing **The Media Side Show** carries five rifles, "exclusive scoops" from tame government sources. The two other *Arms* of the card are stuck into the ground nearby; they are government-approved, or "embedded", journalists. A circus — doubtless that same Circus of Life glimpsed fleetingly throughout these cards — is encamped nearby. Thus is the Circle of Life - symbolized by the Ferris Wheel — made unbroken.

The actual show is, of course, *off to the side of the card*, invisible. In its deceptively simple games, some involving arms, you, Sport, can win a cheesy prize, or not; leaving something of value behind you in any case.

Divinatory Meanings: Attempt, trial balloon. New plans, which may fail. Hope, wish. Alleged. Confidence; shell game. The recruiter's promise. *Reversed:* Advice, counsel, instruction, babbling. Denials. Liberal bloggers, freaky independent voices, wild contradictions. Unnamed sources, unattributed remarks. Plagiarism, sheer fabrication.

VII

ARMS
Six

One of the most celebrated of Presidents, **Theodore Roosevelt** graces our *VI of Arms*. He is portrayed before his Presidency, as a captain in the trumped-up Spanish-American War, waged to supplant the failing Spanish Empire in the Caribbean. What Teddy could have done with those fully-automatic weapons! Even without them, he led a spectacularly well-staged horseback charge up San Juan Hill, on Puerto Rico, which was widely reported, and thus contributed to his fame as well as to the eventual rise of Nuyorican poetry. "T.R."'s rather colorful appearance and manner also drew attention, and his avowed foreign policy, "*Speak softly and carry a big stick*", is still favored in many quarters. First elected in 1900,[cl] T.R.'s "progressive Republicanism" included liberal reforms and enforcement of anti-trust laws at home.

Despite being warlike in regard to US foreign policy, Roosevelt won the Nobel Peace Prize for his efforts to end the Russo-Japanese War. He pushed conservation of America's national resources. He "adopted" an orphan black bear (one wonders if he had shot its mother), inspiring the "Teddy Bear" craze. In other animal antics, Roosevelt refused renomination after two terms in the Oval Office, and sailed for Africa on safari (perhaps the voyage depicted here). After four years away, he tried to regain the Presidency, but was defeated for the Republican nomination by William Taft. Roosevelt then became the candidate of the wild and woolly Progressive, or "Bull Moose", Party. He didn't win, but split the Republican vote, and a Democrat was elected.

Roosevelt was the first President to officially call the White House by that name.[cli]

Divinatory Meanings: Trip or journey. Mission, voyage. To win through difficulties. Bully! *Reversed:* Stalemate, e.g., between Western ranchers and tree-hugging environmentalists. Public declaration, fortuitous press coverage. An unwanted proposal, OR, an offer you can't refuse, OR, "a big stick". OR, a leaky vessel, as in the Progressive Party.

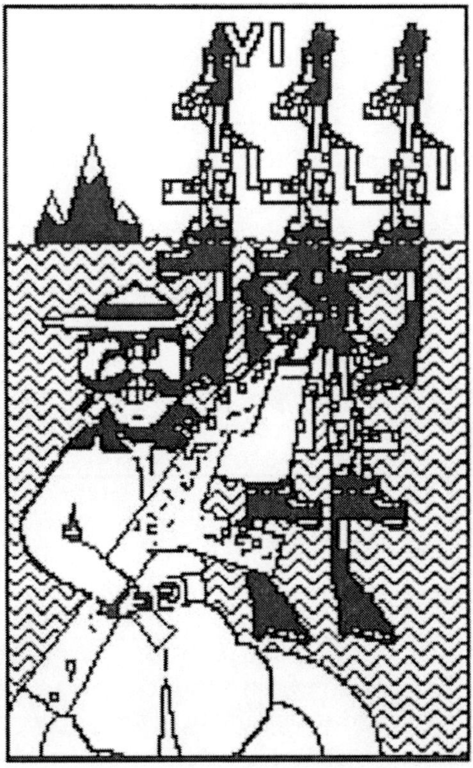
VI

ARMS
Five

James Meredith (1933 – present) the first African-American admitted to the University of Mississippi, in 1962, was escorted to classes by federal marshals sent by then-President John F. Kennedy. Racial riots in Oxford left 2 citizens dead, 48 soldiers injured and 30 marshals with gunshot wounds. Meredith graduated from Ole Miss, studied in Nigeria, and earned a law degree at Columbia University. He led a civil rights march from Memphis, TN to Jackson, MS in 1966, called "The March Against Fear". Meredith was shot and wounded along the march route. (A news photo of the shooting won the Pulitzer Prize for Photography in 1967.)

Not too oddly, Meredith then *stopped wanting to be a civil rights leader*, working for a time as a stockbroker. An active Republican, he was an advisor to unrepentant racist Senator Jesse Helms (**R-NC**). Meredith has said that "he wrote every member of the Senate and House offering his services... in order to gain access to the Library of Congress, and... only Helms replied."[clii] He has run unsuccessfully for Congress several times as a Republican.

"There is considerable enmity between James Meredith and the organized Civil Rights Movement. Meredith once said that, 'Nothing could be more insulting to me than the concept of civil rights. It means perpetual second-class citizenship for me and my kind'."[cliii]

In this card, a disdainful man, in possession of the field, watches his defeated foes skulk away. They have thrown down their *Arms*, while he holds one at the ready, and two more tucked under his left arm.

Divinatory Meanings:: Destruction. Degradation. Dishonor. Infamy. *Reversed:* The same. *Also,* seduction, weakness. Burial.

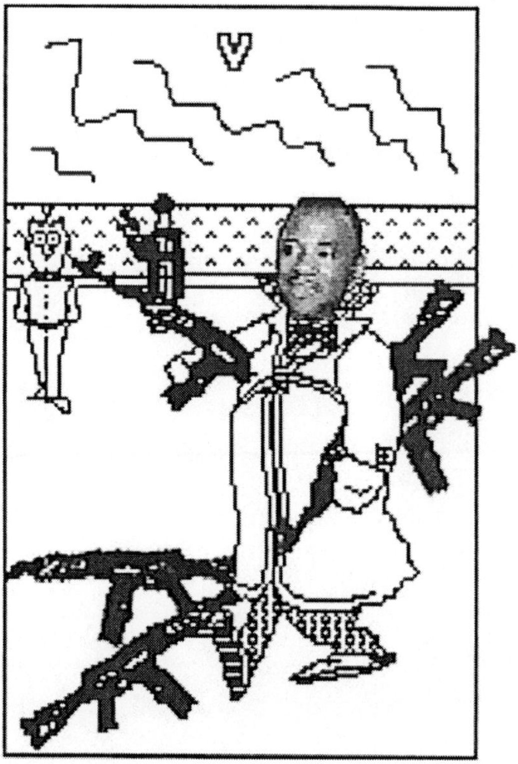
V

ARMS
Four

In a quiet chapel, former President **Dwight D. Eisenhower**, Commander-in-Chief of Allied Forces in World War II, lies at peace, a smile on his pink, grandfatherly face. Five stars show his rank. Four *Arms* form an honor guard, supporting his bier. "Ike's" best legacy was the prescient warning he gave Americans when leaving office in 1960: *beware the military-industrial complex*. Sadly, he hadn't done so himself. US involvement in Vietnam began on his watch. Nor did we heed his advice, possibly because Ike's faith in the Vice-President who he thought would succeed him, the man already known as "Tricky Dick" **Nixon**, had undermined his own credibility.

The innocent, naïve, conformist, boring 1950s were also years of rapid technological change. Eisenhower was the first President to hold a pilot's license, to ride in a jet, and cruise on a submarine.[cliv] Yet the Future which was promised to Americans at that time has not yet come.

Eisenhower is revered by romantics for having cut his and wife Mamie's wedding cake with his sword,[clv] and by libertines for his long-running, open affair with his female Army driver, Kaye Summersby.

Divinatory Meanings: Rest. Replenishment. Retreat. Respite. Repose. Retirement. *Reversed:* Nostalgia. Wise administration, circumspection, caution, testament.

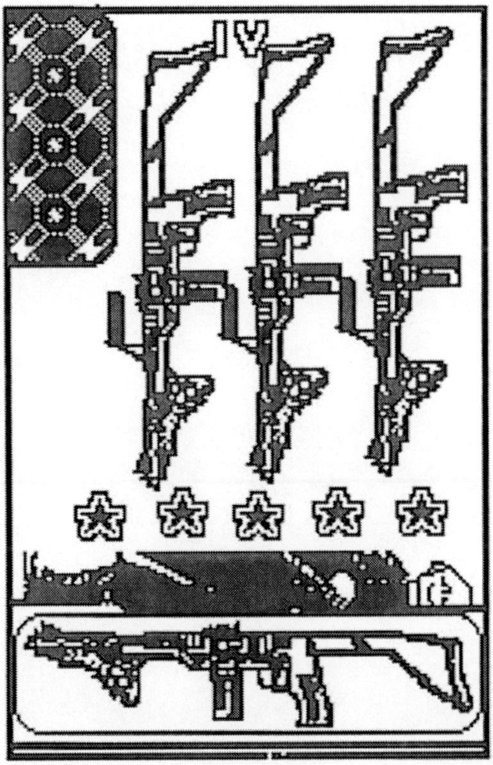
IV

Arms
Three

In this traditional design, three automatic *Arms* pierce a **Purple Heart**, symbolizing those who give their lives in **Patriotic Sacrifice**, whether voluntarily, for love of country, or because they must. Clouds and rain crown the card, the tears of families and friends left behind, seeing dearly-bought Freedom used, abused, and abandoned by a heedless, self-absorbed society. The aftermath of war is war. War is not healthy for children and other living things.

Divinatory Meanings: Absence. Sorrow. Removal. Names on a black wall. "Over there." *Reversed:* Mental alienation, confusion, distraction, loss. Rousting the homeless. Surplus labor. Destitute veterans; shoddy, inadequate medical facilities. National shame. Mercenaries.

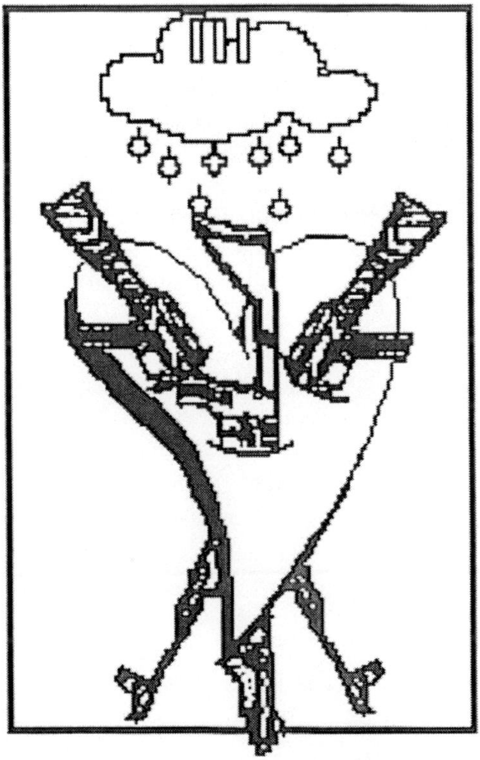

ARMS
Two

If there had been a **Republican Tarot** in the 1960s, '70s, or '80s, this card might have been the *Balanced Ticket*, the once-hallowed tradition of choosing Presidential and Vice-Presidential nominees from different regions, with different constituencies, etc. However, at the beginning of the 21st Century, only one interpretation is possible: that of the **Balanced Budget**. National debt and fiscal folly fueled the 1990's "Republican Revolution", but one-sided globalization, war, and obscene oil profits have led to huge trade deficits and a budget bloated beyond mortal comprehension, as well as to the virtual obliteration of state or regional identities.

In the Circus of Life, an acrobat balances on the high wire; the gawping crowd far below; the bright lights so very near. She balances two *Arms*, held close to her chest. No safety net is seen; perhaps it is merely out of sight, invisible to us as it is to the blindfolded tightrope *artiste*. Recall that spectacular failure gives as much – if not more – satisfaction to onlookers as success.

Divinatory Meanings: Stalemate. Balance; offsetting factors. Harmony. *Reversed:* Cutting programs blindly. Building a silk bridge to nowhere out of a pork earmark. Falsehood, disloyalty. A risky proposition. Bequeathing debt to our great-grandchildren.

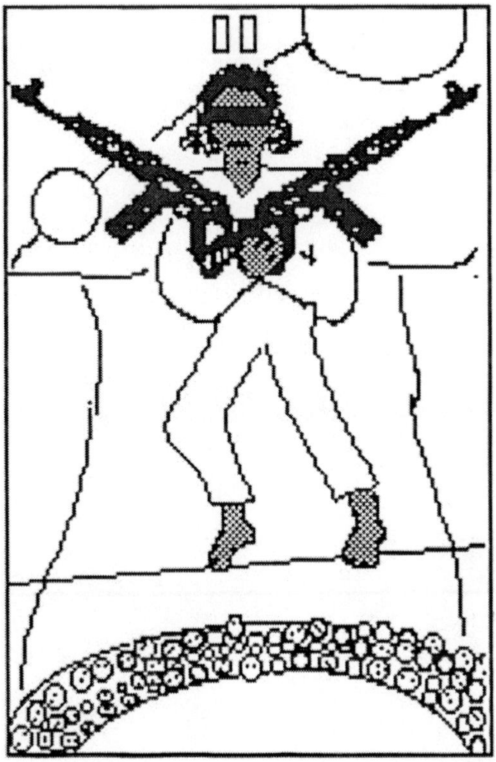
II

Arms
Ace

A muscular Black hand emerges from a cloud, grasping a fully automatic weapon. Caught upon the barrel of the gun is a crown glittering with jewels. Waite writes, "The crown may have a much higher significance than comes usually within the sphere of fortune-telling."[clvi]

However, another Republican, writing much later, Mao Zedong of the Chinese People's Republic, said, "*Power flows from the barrel of a gun*", and it is this interpretation, at its rawest, which best describes the *Ace of Arms*, symbolic of the **Power of the State**.

Divinatory Meanings: Easy solutions. Triumph, power. Success. Racial matters. *Reversed:* Traditionally signifyingt that swords and successes are two-edged: the same results may lead to disaster as easily as to **Victory**. Similarly, there is no such thing as an unloaded gun.

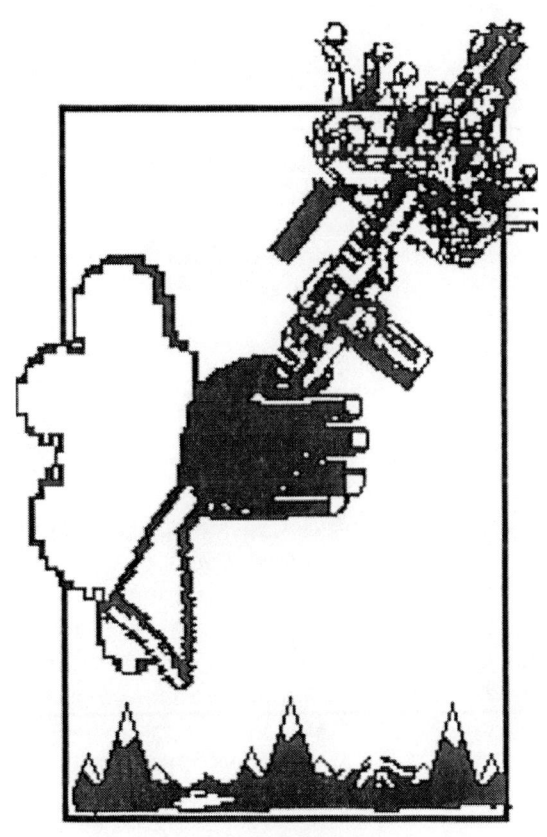

Ace of Arms

Suite of Coins.

COINS
Player

Nelson Wilmarth Aldrich (1841–1915), a descendant of Rhode Island founder Roger Williams, was elected to the US House of Representatives in 1878 for one term, after which he went to the Senate. He was called the "General Manager of the Nation", dominating tariff and monetary policies in the early 20th century.

Aldrich invested in railroads, sugar, and banks. Along with other Americans, he invested in mines and rubber in the Belgian Congo, ignoring slave labor conditions in the colony.

His wife, Abigail Pearce Truman Chapman, was wealthy in her own right, and her ancestors had "come over" on the *Mayflower*. Their daughter, **Abigail**, married the only son of John D. **Rockefeller**. Before going to Congress, Aldrich presided over the Providence, RI, City Council and was Speaker of the Rhode Island House. In the Senate (1881 – 1911), he chaired the Finance Committee. While creating tariffs to keep out foreign agricultural and manufactured goods, Aldrich cut import fees on art, enabling wealthy Americans to bring in European artworks that later became their tax-deductible, charitable gifts to museums.

He introduced a Constitutional amendment to establish an income tax in 1909, although he'd called a similar effort "communistic" 10 years before. A believer in efficiency and science, he studied European **Banks**, finding that Britain, Germany and France had superior banking systems. In 1908 he sponsored the Aldrich-Vreeland Act, creating the National Monetary Commission, and helped plan for an American central bank. In 1913 Woodrow Wilson implemented it as the **Federal Reserve**.

Because of his role in the Senate (*and* his daughter's marriage to Rockefeller, Jr.; *and* his son Winthrop's chairmanship of the Chase National Bank), Aldrich was the most powerful US politician of his day. One grandson, Nelson Aldrich Rockefeller, was Governor of New York, and Vice President under **Gerald Ford** (see *Trump V, The Duffer*); another grandson was Governor of Arkansas at the same time.

Player of Coins

Divinatory Meanings: Business and mathematical aptitude. Experience. Decisiveness. An obedient daughter. *Reversed:* Vice, weakness, instability, tackiness, perversity, contrariness, avarice, meanness. Corruption. Using any means to achieve one's end.

COINS
Lady

Abby Aldrich Rockefeller (1874–1948), socialite, philanthropist, and second-generation matriarch of the Rockefeller family, was the daughter of Senator **Nelson Wilmarth Aldrich (R-RI)**, and the former Abby Pearce Truman Chapman. Her early education was with Quaker governesses. Later, she attended Miss Abbott's School for Young Ladies. She graduated and made her social debut in 1893. In 1894 she sailed to Liverpool, beginning a lifetime of extensive travel.

That same year, she met future husband John Davison Rockefeller, Jr., sole son of oilman-philanthropist John D. Rockefeller. They had a long engagement, including a trip to Cuba on President McKinley's yacht. Papparazzi were not allowed! The wedding was a major society event of the Gilded Age, with 1000 elite guests. Their nine-story mansion, the largest in New York City at the time, became home to six children, and the seat of a business/philanthropic/banking/real estate dynasty. Abby collected paintings, watercolors, and drawings by contemporary artists: van Gogh, Degas, Matisse, Picasso, Cezanne, and Toulouse-Lautrec. She created a suite of rooms in her home to exhibit her growing collection. Visitors took an elevator directly to the 7th floor. Other collectors followed her lead. She became a prominent patroness of modern art and the driving force behind New York's Museum of Modern Art, which opened in 1929 nine days after the Wall Street crash. The Abby Aldrich Rockefeller Print Room at MoMA houses her gift of 1600 prints.

Dedicated to the advancement of **Women**, Mrs. Rockefeller was an active clubwoman. Along with her husband, she served on the board of the International House of New York. For decades she worked with the YWCA's National Board. She chaired the Grace Dodge Hotel committee, organizing construction of a "decent" hotel for women in government, as well as visitors to Washington. In the 1920s, Abby and John helped fund the restoration of Colonial Williamsburg, VA, a living history museum and major tourist attraction. The Abby Aldrich Rockefeller Folk Art Museum is located there.

Divinatory Meanings: Opulence, generosity, security, liberty. Abundance. Compassionate conservatism. *Reversed:* Suspense, mistrust, suspicion of the unfamiliar. Bad Impressionism; fishy *hors d'oeurves*.

Lady of Coins

COINS
Knave

Ulysses S. Grant was the first general in the US Civil War to coordinate an offense in multiple theaters. At Ft. Donelson, the surrender of 12,000 Rebels earned him the nickname "Unconditional Surrender" in the first big Union victory of the war. **Lincoln** made him major general of volunteers. He forced Confederate Gen. Robert E. Lee to defend his capitol, Richmond, Virginia. In April, 1865, the Union army broke through the lines there, and Lee surrendered.

Grant became President in 1868, the first to serve two full terms since Andrew Jackson 40 years earlier. Radical Reconstruction had built a strong, patronage-based Republican Party in the South and curbed Ku Klux Klan violence. However, as Reconstruction fervor faded, Grant watched Democratic "Redeemers" take over. When Southern leaders begged for help, he said, "*the whole public is tired of these... outbreaks,*" and said that state militias should handle problems, not the Army.

Grant blocked civil service and internal party reforms. In the Whiskey Ring scandal, $3 million was stolen from the government. Grant's private secretary was indicted but received a Presidential pardon. War Secretary William Belknap took bribes. Grant let him resign, escaping conviction. But the financial Panic of 1873 threw the nation into a depression Grant couldn't jolly it out of. Often ranked among the worst presidents for his tolerance of corruption, his reputation has improved somewhat due to his early support for voting rights for African Americans, in a proposed annexation of the largely black island of Santo Domingo, which eventually came to naught.

"Stalwart" Republicans (businessmen, veterans, Methodists) tried to nominate Grant for a third term, but the nod went to James Garfield. In 1881, Grant lost his money in an investment banking scheme. He found he had throat cancer.[clvii] He and his family were destitute. US Presidents then had no pensions; and Grant had given up his military pension as President. Mark Twain offered to publish his memoirs. Grant finished them only days before he died. Twain called the book, "the most remarkable work of its kind since the *Commentaries of Julius Caesar.*" Grant has been called "the greatest general of his age and one of the greatest strategists of any age." His tomb, in New York City, is the

Knave of Coins

largest mausoleum in North America.[clviii]. On our card, the Knave of Coins rides an iron horse on the fast track of capitalist expansion.

Divinatory Meanings: Maturity. Persistence. Attrition, scorched earth. Serviceability, utility, responsibility. Methodical. *Reversed:* Inertia, idleness. Carelessness. Fermentation of spirits. Lack of determination or direction. Unimaginative. Discouragement, placidity.

COINS
Varlet

Arch-Liberal, first Republican President **Thomas Jefferson** (1801-1809), admires a symbol of his suite within the stately rooms of Monticello. Spreading oaks are seen through the window. The Varlet rests one foot upon a velvet footstool, as though he might have a little Captain in him; one hand rests on the head of someone who may be kneeling before him. The person's slender neck, curly hair and dusky complexion suggest that this may be Sally Hemings, Jefferson's slave and mistress, the mother of several of his children. Jefferson, like other Founding Fathers, grew cannabis hemp; unlike the others, he kept a pet grizzly bear at his estate, and trained a mockingbird to follow him around the place.[clix]

Divinatory Meanings: Study, scholarship, reflection. Favorable opinion. Good news, or a messenger. *Reversed:* Prodigality, expense, liberality, dissipation. Unrealistic. Failure to recognize facts. Illogical. Bad news.

Varlet of Coins

Coins
Ten

This adaptation of a traditional design depicts the *Golden Years*. A **Family** group stands beneath a brick arch, behind a stout fence. The man and woman seem pensive. The child looks curiously through the fence, where an elderly man is being accosted by a snarling dog, which may represent a fixed income. A smaller dog -- perhaps real property or an annuity? -- loiters near the fence. Many of the card's *Coins* are aloft, with wings spread, as if they are flying away.

Divinatory Meanings: Security, safety. Sun City. Gain. Family decisions. Pension. *Reversed:* Warehousing of the elderly. Discontinuance of federal nursing home standards. A fatality. Loss, robbery, hazard.

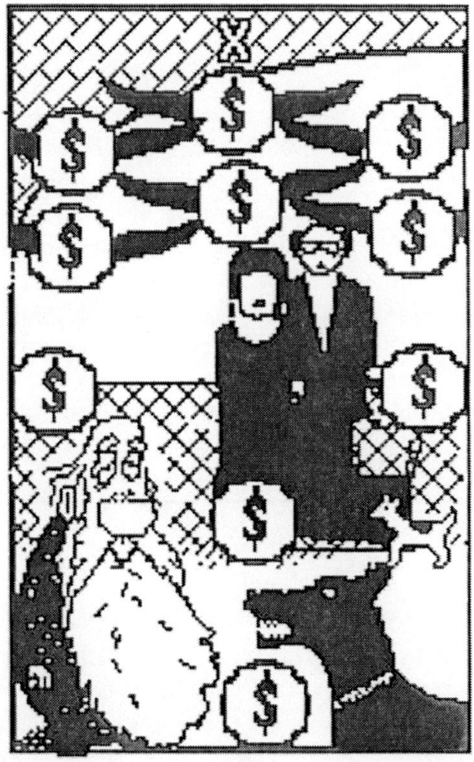
X

COINS
Nine

US Senator (**R-TX**) **Kay Bailey Hutchison** embodies the smug snugness of the *IX of Coins*. Elegantly attired, she welcomes the Inquirer (and silent, illegal migrants) to a charming if pesticide-laden arbor on a rich estate. An extinct owl, formerly residing in East Texas' endangered Piney Woods, depends from her arm. Woman in Her Aspect as Cheerleader.

In 1972, Hutchison was elected to the Texas Legislature. She then worked for the National Transportation Safety Board (1976 -- 1978). She ran for the US House in Dallas, but lost the primary, and temporarily left politics to be a bank executive and businesswoman. She became Texas State Treasurer (1990 -- 1993), then ran for the US Senate against Sen. Bob Krueger (**D-TX**), to complete the last two years of Sen. Lloyd Bentsen's (**D-TX**) term. (Bentsen had become **Bill Clinton**'s Treasury Secretary. Krueger served until a sub was elected.) A field of 24 sought the job. Hutchison beat Krueger in a run-off to become the first female Texas Senator. She promised to serve a maximum two terms, supporting **Term Limits**. She said term limits should cover all Senators, even Phil Gramm (**R-TX**), elected in 1984, re-elected in 1990, and a power in the Senate until 2002. Term limits didn't pass, however; and Hutchison now says she won't voluntarily leave office without such legislation, as that would hurt Texas in the seniority-driven Senate.

In 2006, Hutchison got more *Coins* from oil and gas companies than anyone else in Congress. She supports drilling in the Arctic National Wildlife Refuge. She voted to exclude oil and gas smokestacks from Environmental Protection Agency mercury regulations. In 1999, she voted against funds for renewable and solar energy, although she now says she supports alternative energy. The League of Conservation Voters gave Hutchison a zero -- *the lowest possible score* -- in the 104th Congress.

Touted as a possible Vice-Presidential candidate in 2008, especially if **Hillary Clinton** is tapped for the top spot by Democrats, Hutchison is also a possible candidate for Governor of Texas in 2010.[clx]

Divinatory Meanings: Prudence, safety. Plenty. Accomplishment. Love of nature. *Reversed:* Roguery. Deception. A voided project. Possible loss of valued friendship or treasured possession, e.g., Endangered Species Act.

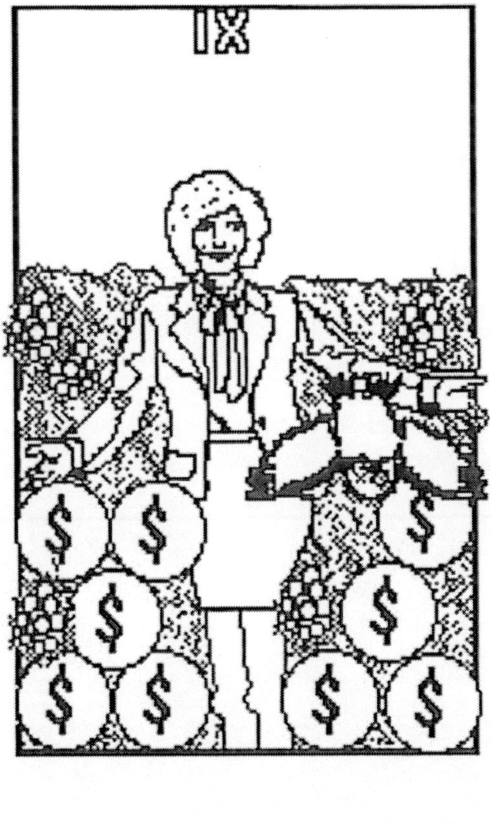
IX

Coins
Eight

The American Free Enterprise System/Free American Labor. Dissatisfaction, layoffs, speedups, strikes, runaway shops, corrupt officials, stolen pension funds... in this complex interplay, simple pride in a job well done is a costly emotional liability.

The *VIII of Coins* depicts a workingman at his bench, using specialized tools with skill and care. He is not, of course, at his actual swing-shift job, but preparing for an upcoming week-end crafts fair in his home workshop; he may make a few extra *Coins* there, and it keeps him home nights, and out of the bars.

Divinatory Meanings: Trade schools. Apprenticeship. Productivity, assembly. Work, employment, commission. Skill with one's hands. Personal effort. *Reversed:* Vanity, frustrated ambition. Make-work. Featherbedding. Lack of innovation. Hypocrisy, flattery, intrigue. Affirmative action quotas met for display purposes only. If the Querent is a woman, the Glass Ceiling.

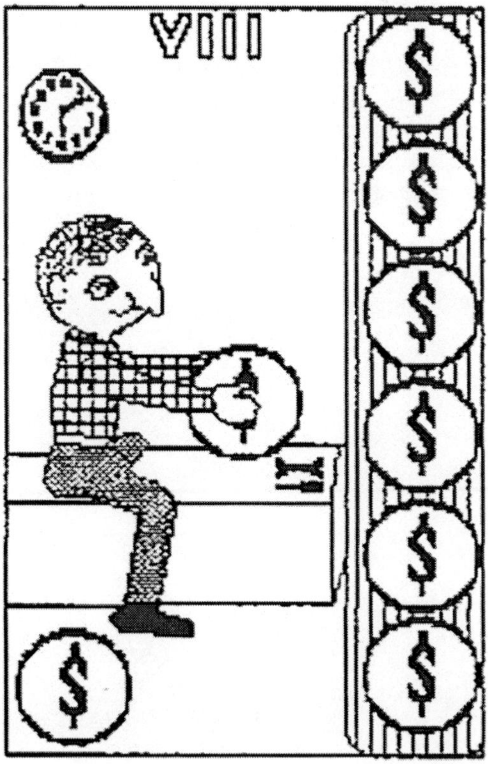
VIII

COINS
Seven

A top-hatted banker of the **Federal Reserve** -- no doubt a member of **Mr. Aldrich**'s set? -- tends his investments. It is easy to see his satisfaction with the task, as the greenery bursts with shiny *Coin*-fruit. When one has the power to print money, money literally *does* grow on trees!

Divinatory Meanings: Ingenuity, enterprise. Growth. A harvest to come. Money, business, barter. Wealth. *Reversed:* Imprudent actions. Loss of money. Unwise investment. Warning against lending money to pornographers, arms dealers, drug kingpins, shiftless relatives.

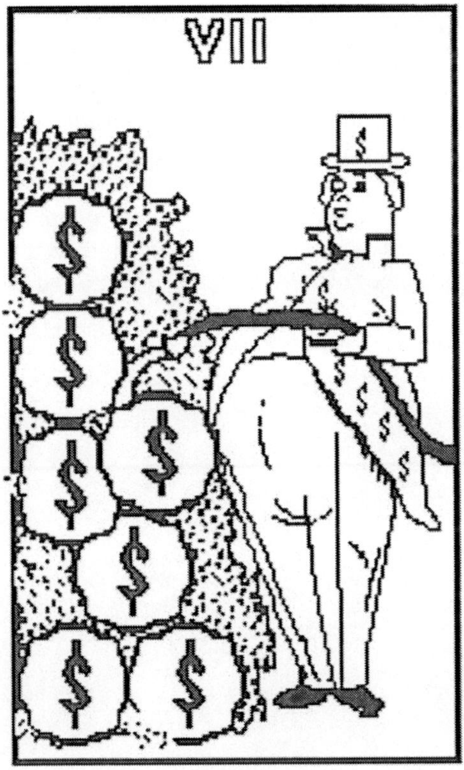
VII

COINS
Six

A bored woman behind a desk vigilantly ignores, delays and hampers the applications of the hapless, gormless, needy and distressed patrons of the **Welfare System**. It was a testimony to her good luck alone that she had a job, and she knows it; but her good luck ran out as the Republican Congress in 1996 forced the dissolution of the federal welfare system and returned responsibility for the poor to the several states. Perhaps this experienced bureaucratic obstacle has now gotten a job with some compassionate conservative charity. On the other hand, she may have joined the ranks of the needy.

Divinatory Meanings: Private generosity to the worthy poor. Charity. Gifts. Material gain. *Reversed:* Desire, greed, envy, illusion. Bad debts, unpaid loans, utilities cut off. Enabling dysfunctional behavior.

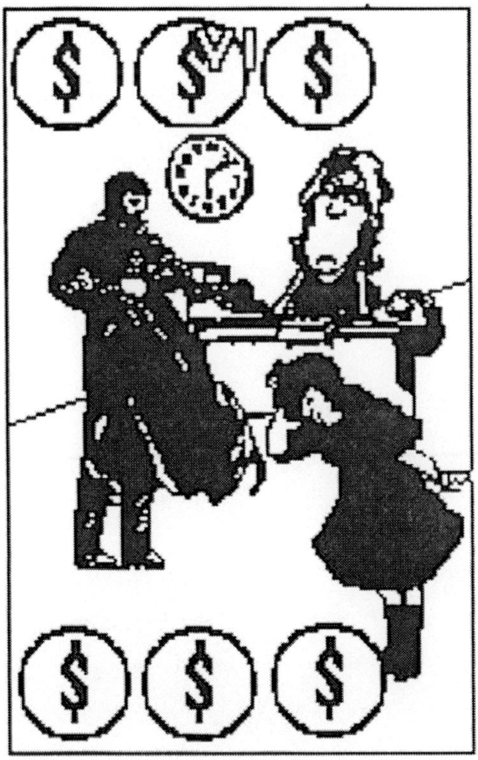

COINS
Five

Healthcare providers, seen in a perfect storm of regulatory paper work and misinformation, represent the always-precariously funded **Medicare** and **Medicaid**. Behind them, seemingly unattainable, shines the illuminated window of a single-payer system, with its potential savings seen as gleaming *Coins* of light.

Divinatory Meanings: Material troubles. Disability; iatrogenic disease. Impoverishment; malpractice insurance, medical debt. *Reversed:* Disorder, ruin, discord, hazardous waste. Pharmaceutical industry influence; junkets; cruises; office supplies with names of pills on them. Fallacy. *Or,* reversal of a bad trend.

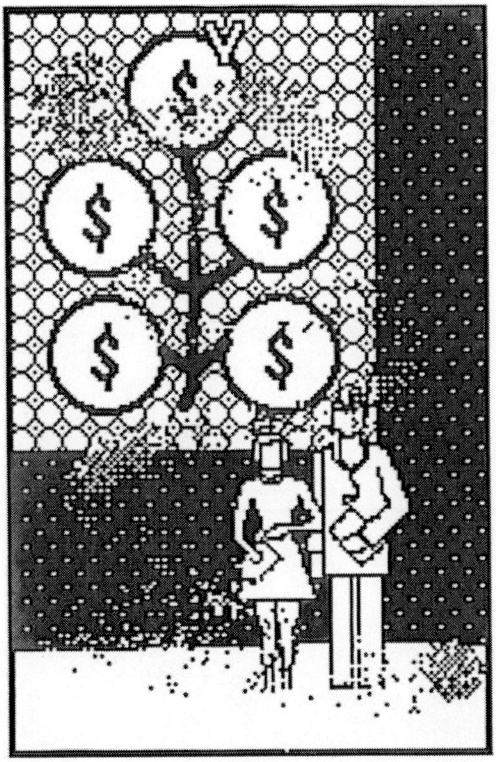

COINS
Four

The **Social Security System**, an elderly man in a wheelchair, balances one *Coin* on his head and clasps another in his arms; two others form the wheels of his chair. *He doesn't believe a word you say.*

Divinatory Meanings: Keeping what one has. Entitled. Miserly, a hoarder, skinflint. *Reversed:* Suspense, rumor, delay, opposition to further gain. Spendthrift. Bankruptcy. The kids are *not* alright.

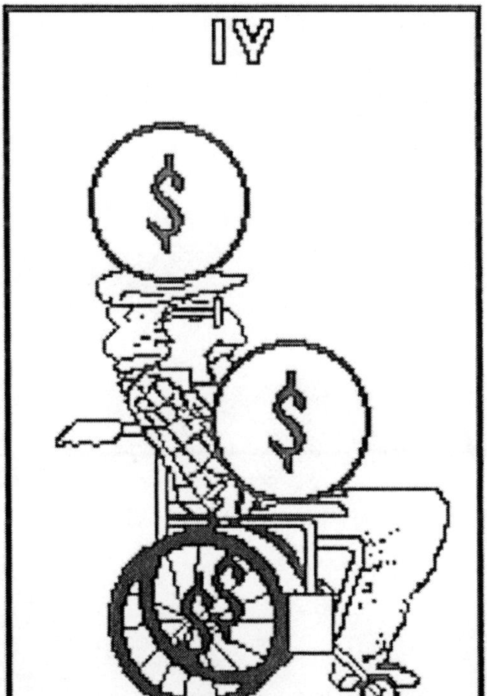
IV

COINS
Three

Public Education is an ideological battlefield between those who would teach the young to think, and those who would sell them *their very thoughts*. In textbooks and curricula, in school voucher plans, the **Christian Right** chips away at the barrier between Church and State, erected at great cost by, among other events, the American Revolution. Colleges and military lower entry standards to meet the "dumbed down" products of our schools. But test scores (see *Varlet of Bushes*) aren't as useful as problem-solving skills; nor is teaching that "everyone is a winner", rather than that "everyone can learn". Early 1900s school tests found on the Internet illuminate our educational devolution. Yet today's Youth are no stupider than yesteryear's. The **Mass Media**, including the Internet, have become our teachers, and we their suckling, moonstruck calves. Schools are built to contain bodies, not to open minds. Here, education continues its downhill slide, while corporate school "sponsors" count their *Coins*.

Divinatory Meanings: Marketplace of ideas. One against the mob. Glory. Mastery. Reward. Rank, dignity. Are you smarter than a 5th grader? *Reversed:* Mediocre, petty, sloppy. Money problems. Public rejection. Voted off the island. Simon says you're a loser. Falling scores; standards. "*All in all, you're just a – 'Nother brick in the wall.*"[clxi]

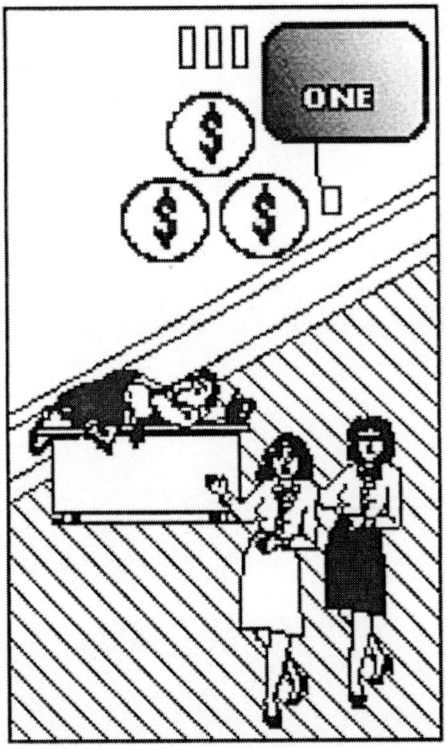
ONE

COINS
Two

A clown, representing **Opinion Polls**, soft-shoes across the *II of Coins*, juggling the *Coins* within a ribbon of flexible statistics. Note the resemblance of this ribbon to the symbol for Infinity, first seen with the **Magician** and later with **Strength**. This is also the final manifestation of our Circus metaphor. Two trial balloons float up and down nearby, the positives and negatives of public perception, the margin of error in any poll. The green balloon says "Go"; the red one, "Stop". May represent a call to action, as in, "*Dare to juggle, dare to spin!*"[clxii]

Divinatory Meanings: Gaiety. Popularity. Recreation. News or messages in writing. Statistics. *Reversed:* Enforced gaiety. Pretended enjoyment. Computer simulations; virtual reality; focus groups. Obstacles, set-backs. Margin of error. Damned statistics.

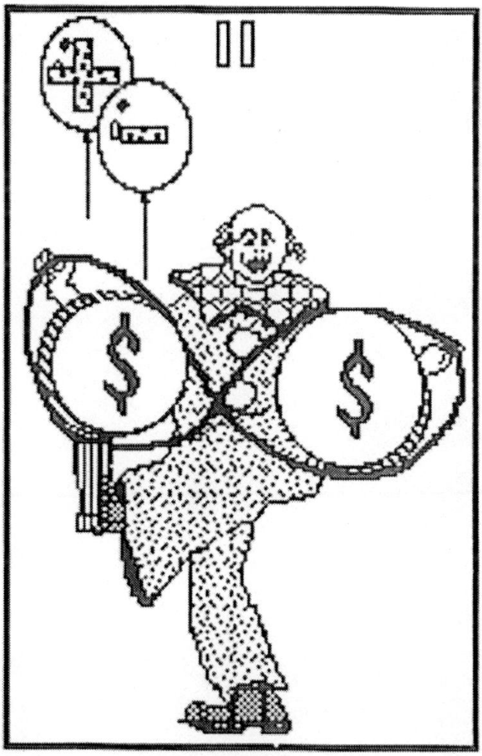
II

COINS
Ace

A hand issuing from a cloud holds a *Coin*. A pathway through a garden leads to an arched gate; beyond it is seen only an undefined brilliance. The card is **Capitalism**, which is *not* synonymous with Democracy! In capitalism, it is necesary always for the future to be brighter; for the grass to be made greener using a new, improved fertilizer; and for that fertilizer to cost you a lot of green. Eventually, the future becomes so bright, you have to wear shades.[clxiii]

Divinatory Meanings: Perfect contentment. Having your cake and eating it, too. Ecstasy. Quick intelligence. Gold, valuable items, tribute. Class distinction. *Reversed:* Evil intelligence. The evil of great wealth. Prosperity without happiness. Corruption by money. Unrealistic expectations. Pie in the sky.

Ace of Coins

§ 3

Conclusion as to the Greater Key(e)s

"The Key interface is the top-level interface for all keys. It defines the functionality shared by all key objects. All keys have three characteristics." -- Java™ 2 Platform, Std. Ed. v1.4.2

While there will be no attempt here to present a complete or even remotely balanced history of Republicanism – a slimmer volume would be needed for that – I shall do what Waite did not: draw examples of what he calls the *Three Worlds*, of Divinity, of the Macrocosm, and the Microcosm, through well-known Republican avatars and associations. However, determining what each of these terms may describe, and assignment of the persons and locations described below to one or another world, must be left to the Seeker, in order that such individual meditation produce its deepest rewards.[clxiv]

Francis Scott Key (1780-1843), son of an American Revolutionary officer, practiced law in Frederick City, Maryland, then moved to Washington, where he became the lead Attorney for the **District of Columbia**.

When the **British** invaded Washington in 1814, **Gen. Ross** and **Adm. Cockburn**, with their officers, made their headquarters at the plantation of Key's friend, **Dr. William Beanes**, whom they held prisoner. Key resolved to free him, and **President James Madison** ordered that a ship be placed at his service, and US agent **John Skinner** accompany him. The British finally consented to Beanes' release, but detained the party until after their pending attack on **Baltimore**. Key and Skinner watched the battle, under guard, from their own ship. The American flag at **Fort McHenry** could be seen through the night by the light of battle, but by dawn, the firing ceased, and the hostages watched to see which flag flew over the fort. Key expressed his joy when he saw that it had not fallen by writing *The Star-Spangled Banner*, later adopted as the US national anthem, gaining him a deserved reputation for sadism among both soloists and spectatorrs at sporting events.[clxv] While Key lived and died before the advent of Republicanism, the song he penned has become, along with the Flag, a litmus test for Party faithful. In 2006, a Spanish version, sung by immigrants, added new fuel to the indignation of "English-only" advocates, apparently unaware that Key's song has long been translated into dozens of languages worldwide.

Alan Keyes (1950 --), former diplomat, conservative political activist, was a member of the Republican Party until 2006. Keyes worked for the US **State Department** as a protegé of UN Ambassador **Jeanne Kirkpatrick**. In 1983, **President Reagan** appointed him the US' first Black UN Ambassador. Keyes dutifully defended Reagan's opposition to economic sanctions against apartheid **South Africa**. In 1988, he was nominated for one of **Maryland**'s US **Senate** seats, and received 38% of the vote. He ran again four years later, winning just 29%.

Keyes sought the Republican Presidential nomination in 1996. During the primaries, he was briefly detained by **Atlanta** police when he tried to force his way into a debate to which he was not invited. He ran again in 2000. He hung in the race after the early primaries and met the two leading candidates, **John McCain** and **George W. Bush**, in nationally-televised debates. Eager to win young voters, he leapt into a mosh pit of body-surfers on **Michael Moore**'s television show, *The Awful Truth*.

Keyes was criticized when he said **Jesus** wouldn't vote for 2008 Presidential contender, and Keyes' fellow African-American, **Barack Obama**, since as a State Senator Obama (**D-IL**) voted against legislation "protecting" infants who might survive **Abortion**. Keyes was also criticized for saying that homosexuality is based on "selfish hedonism." Asked if **Mary Cheney**, Vice President **Dick Cheney**'s lesbian daughter, was a selfish hedonist, Keyes replied, *"Of course she is. That goes by definition."* Keyes' daughter, **Maya**, is also a lesbian woman.

Keyes had a syndicated radio program, *The Alan Keyes Show: America's Wake-Up Call*, in **Virginia**. In 2002, he hosted a television talk show on the **MSNBC** cable channel. The network claimed declining ratings led to the show's demise. Others pointed to pressure by groups such as pro-**Gay** organizations and the **Palestinian lobby**. The show often discussed priests accused in **Roman Catholic Church Sex Abuse Scandals**. Keyes now serves on the Board of Directors of the **Catholic League**.[clxvi]

Florida Keys. As the sun rose over No Name Key, **Florida**, one April day in 1961, **CIA** operatives prepared for what would soon become one of America's most infamous military blunders, the **Bay of Pigs**. While that losing effort was surpassed in later years, worse may be yet to come for the Florida Keys:

"Nobody much was watching... when... experts [testified] that the Florida Keys and chunks of **Miami-Dade County** could be under the **Atlantic** before the end of this century because of rising sea levels. 'Climate change is arguably the biggest threat to... Florida,' said futurist **Clement Bezold** in a presentation to the **Century Commission for a Sustainable Florida**. And because of its long coastline, 'Florida is... the state with the most to lose from climate change and is doing the least about it.'

"Meanwhile, nine coal plants are in some stage of planning by Florida utilities -- including plants at the edge of the **Everglades**.

"This is where government actually matters. The **Florida Public Service Commission** has to authorize any generating plant... But the PSC's political appointees have rebuffed environmental issues because their jurisdiction is economic. Never mind that environmental issues are economic ones."[clxvii]

Let it also be noted here that Florida was a "key", and hotly contested, state in the 2000 Presidential election, and but recall what has been said herein of the *Minor Arcana,* and the *Suite of Bushes* in particular, to grasp what was unlocked in its wielding!

§4
A Note on The Joker

To the best of my knowledge, this is the only tarot deck to date including, as common card decks do, a *Joker*. Indeed, given the money-grubbing character of my enterprise – and if I were trying to market a printed Deck rather than give away a Virtual one! -- it would be preferable for me if a careless coffee spill or pet accident were to render an entire Deck unuseable and defunct, requiring immediate replacement!

Yet such a course, perfectly justifiable under the tenets of unrestrained Capital, would have deprived you, Faithful Reader, of an extraordinary Republican personage, and one of the most extraordinary claims ever voiced within our Constitutional government!

I refer, of course, to **Richard Cheney**, 46th Vice-President (2001-present), of whose rise to power much may be read in earlier pages, and who, in 2007, asserted that his office was *not part of the Executive Branch*, and therefore exempt from even the limited Congressional scrutiny imposed upon Presidents. Dubbed the "Black Branch" by *Doonesbury* creator Garry Trudeau,[clxviii] this claim will, it is devoutly to be hoped, be Cheney's last claim to fame, along with his penchant for vacationing in "undisclosed locations", getting his henchmen out of prison sentences, and his work on behalf of Halliburton Energy Services, one of the **Multinational Corporations** profiting most from US involvement in **Iraq** and the so-called "war on terror".

Arguably the mot powerful Vice President in the nation's history, Cheney is also the first sitting Veep to shoot another person with a gun since Aaron Burr nicked Alexander Hamilton in their 1804 duel. Cheney wounded an associate – *carelessly and accidentally* -- while hunting. Yet there is nothing careless or accidental about *The Joker*.

Divinatory: There is no fixed meaning. Adaptable to changing situations, *The Joker*'s power is in his lack of definition. Use the card as you like, *The Joker* has the last laugh!

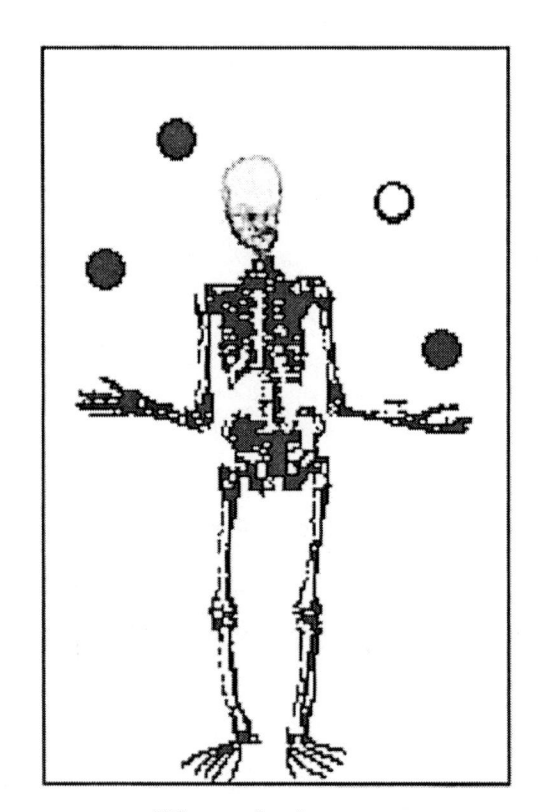

The Joker

§ 5
THE ART OF TAROT DIVINATION

As to the process of "reading" the cards designed to accompany this book, it is here that I tire at last of endless meanderings, and shall present but two of many methods of divination which may be practiced, and those without repeating what has been said clearly and well by many before me on the necessity of washing one's hands before and after using the cards; of making one's mind a complete blank, insofar as possible, throughout the entire process; and of learning to shuffle the cards with some degree of skill and finesse. After shuffling, it is often required of the Seeker to touch or cut the cards. Some Practitioners instruct the Seeker to select, from among all the cards, the one with which he or she feels the strongest rapport. Others will simply draw the first card after the shuffle and cut, turn it face up, and designate it the Significator, proceeding to spread the other cards in a manner shown in a following section, or in any other of the practitioner's preference.

Questions or issues remaining after a first reading may be pursued by continuing through the deck, repeating the pattern of the first spread – that is, laying down a second Significator and so forth for each succeeding position in the layout – or in some other manner which better suits one's inclination.

Regardless of the method used, the skill of the practitioner may lie not so much in patterns but in patter; owing less to otherworldly revelation than to empathy. In this way a good Tarot reader may resemble the successful public official, able periodically to convince a majority of voters that he or she has their best interests at heart; yea, *knows what those interests may be*, even if they have not previously been articulated. As the most respected leaders lead by following, so the most respected readers empower their clients to discover what may be causing disorder or discomfort in their lives, and to find their own paths to change.

Perhaps the Seeker who has read so far in this tome will now understand why I have concerned myself with this subject, even at the risk of writing about divination by cards, or by opinion polls. The Future, perhaps, may not be predicted, but it may be ridden out by those who wish not to repeat the Past. Heed the message of *Time*, Seeker, and know, that in understanding is our only salvation!

§ 6
AN ANCIENT CELTIC METHOD OF DIVINATION

The cards are dealt in the order and pattern shown. "Celtic Cross" method:

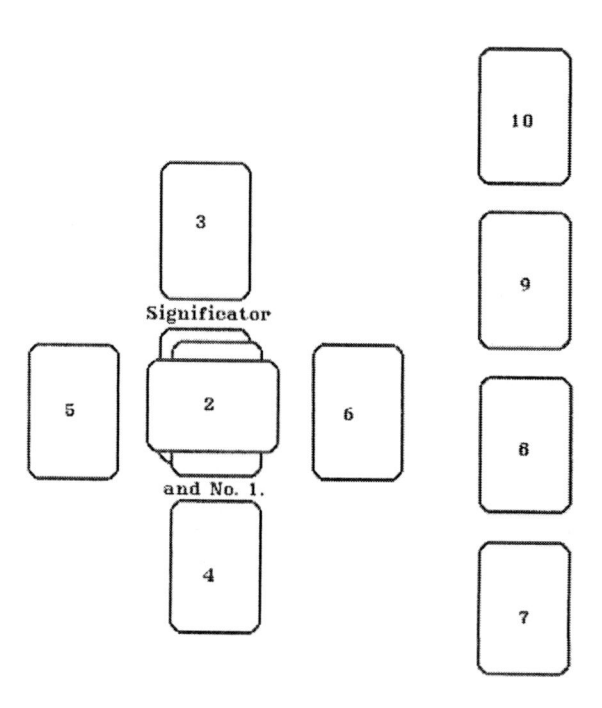

The Inquirer (Significator; how the Seeker sees him/herself).
1. What covers him (the current situation).
2. What crosses him (opposing forces).
3. What crowns him (the best outcome of the situation).
4. What is beneath him (the root of the situation).
5. What is behind him (the immediate past).
6. What is before him (the immediate future).
7. Himself (the Seeker's position in the matter).
8. His house (the Seeker's position beyond the matter).
9. Hopes and fears.
10. What will come (the outcome of the matter).

§ 7
THE POLITICS-AS-LIFE METHOD OF READING THE TAROT CARDS

The cards are dealt in the order and pattern shown. This Novel method, shown here for the first time anywhere, may be especially useful to those who are from time to time exhorted by deluded friends to seek public office. Also called the "Triple Cross" spread:

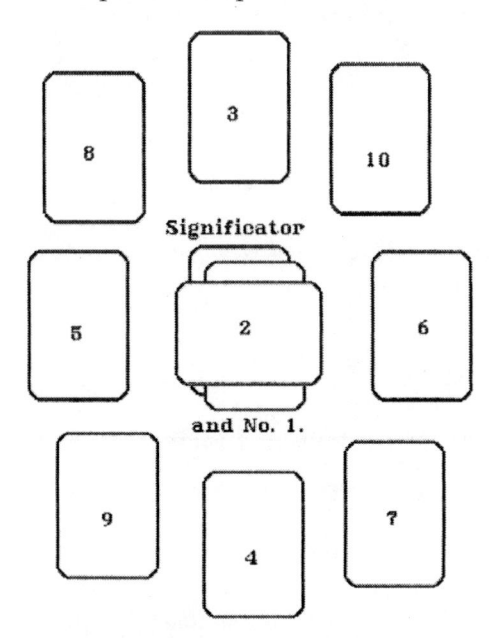

The Candidate (Significator)
1. Who owns him?
2. Who opposes him?
3. Who knows him?
4. Who owes him?
5. Who backs him?
6. Who fronts him?
7. What is his advertising budget?
8. Who does he own?
9. Where is he at?
10. Where is he going? (the outcome of the matter)

Afterword : Confession

As my work here draws to a close, after what must seem as interminable a time to the Reader as to the Author, I ask your indulgence as I offer amends to the gifted Tarot readers and other psychics who have, on occasion, read the cards, runes and stars for me or for my loved ones, to our astonishment and frequent benefit.

Some years ago my family was rent by a disaster as dreadful in our lives as the *Watergate* in the life of the Republican Party. It was then that circumstances forced me to set early work on this book aside, where from the Presidency of **George H.W. Bush** to that of our current Leader, **George "Dubya" Bush**,[clxix] it lay fallow. For several years my life was such that any opportunity to gain insight into the Way was welcome. During this time, two women, unacquainted with and unaware of each other, were able, for me and for others torn by The Situation, to provide comforting assurances, gained from the cards, that everything would – eventually – turn out alright. And indeed it does, as Unfinished Creation continues to unfold.

Yet both of these Readers were friends; both knew the outlines of our quest, and the skeptical will surely remain so, especially as I may not provide any details of their insights.

But there was more. Someone I had never met, an astrologer 1000 miles away, did natal charts for me and two dear ones, knowing nothing more of us or our relationships than our birth dates, then told me, *"In the legal matter with which you are concerned, there is something concealed, something you don't yet know about; when you find out about it everything can be resolved."* And in a steamy Central American town, a tiny Mayan woman spread her worn, ancient cards, of a style I'd never seen before, and have not seen since, in a pattern also novel to me but as structured and practiced as any, across her kitchen table. Touching several in turn and talking them over under her breath in no language I knew, she peered most closely at an oddity even I could discern: all four Knights were out there, clustered near the center of the spread. After a few moments she raised her sparkling black eyes to me, laid all my secrets bare, and gave me a gift to protect against a clear and present peril.

What it was she gave me need not be revealed,[clxx] but what may be known is this: when what we didn't know came to light, a certain legal matter could be resolved, and was. Until that day, my family was safe, though each of us walked dangerous paths. I have been of a materialist bent all my life, partial to analysis, facts, and things I can see for myself, but during this time, in what I think of now as the **Lions**' den, we were surely in the hands of a Higher Power than any government may wield.

So I will end this little satire on a serious note after all, albeit one of some small Mystery, in the sincere hope that none who read this work, who themselves practice the Art of the Tarot, who benefit from it, or from any other Path to Knowledge, mistake satire for disrespect or material aims for disbelief. Indeed it is only through the deepest respect for the Mystery of Life, of which Tarot is, after all, but a symbol, that I am able to use it as a reckless vehicle for running down a more modern construct, one for which I have considerably less respect, and in which I have no confidence at all.

Here is a final confession: Like **Pat Buchanan**, I was a Young Republican during the 1964 Presidential attempt of Senator **Barry Goldwater (R-AZ)**, although I was then too young to vote; and I cannot yet bring myself to lampoon that earnestly deluded man. Furthermore I have, through the years, voted for honorable and honest Republicans in several jurisdictions, as I've had occasion to do so, although none of those votes have been for a Republican Presidential candidate, and none of this year's Republican aspirants for nomination grace these pages. *If* Democrats, predictably, in 2008, a year in which they feel entitled to **Victory**, choose only the most "experienced," most moderate, most conciliatory, *least specific* candidates available, and *if* pigs should concurrently fly and Republicans nominate darkhorse, sometime-Libertarian Rep. **Ron Paul (R-TX)**, Fortune might yet favor **Republican Victory**! About this possibility, the cards are silent.

More than one species of Republican
is found within the Big Tent.

Bibliographic Note

Many sources, credited below, have been consulted in compiling this work. I shall make absolutely no attempt, as Arthur Edward Waite did, to list major works on the Tarot, or on Republicanism, or any other topic; today the interested Seeker can find more than S/He wants to know by "googling"[clxxi] virtually any word or phrase. The transformation of the Internet, or World Wide Web, from a cranky, idiosyncratic luxury to a primary means of communication and information exchange for millions of people *worldwide* occurred between the time this work was begun and its completion, and I would be remiss if I did not acknowledge its influence. In its early stages, **The Republican Tarot** was something of a lark, in addition to being patently absurd, but as I dug into it, and the research which would be required to begin to do justice to the conceit became clear, I somewhat despaired of seeing the end of it. Yet when I returned to it after a lengthy hiatus, advances in what is available to the Electronic Seeker allowed a relatively painless finish. Having access to such wealth of information *at any hour* also played a part, as we writers seem to function best between 11 pm and 4 am,[clxxii] when few physical libraries are open; or in marathon 3-day spurts, whilst most bricks-and-books libraries like to occasionally clear the carrels.

In particular, I have relied upon **Wikipedia**, The Free Encyclopedia, and its thousands of contributors. While it may be true, as **Wikipedia** itself says, that many scholars do not accept encyclopedic citations alone, birth and death dates, years in office, and the order in which particular scandals unfolded were most easily and reliably found in this ever-evolving compilation of democratic knowledge and opinion. And after all, mine is no scholarly work, but one of entertainment and satire, and if the Reader has gained aught of value within, it is unlikely to be from the bare historical bones upon which it is based, but from their juxtaposition with that other arcane pursuit, divination with cards.

The rise of Internet-based, print-on-demand publishing, and electronic books, has also materially enabled the public debut of a work quixotic at best in its potential commercial appeal. There is no warehouse full of mouldering, remaindered copies of this work, nor of the cards meant to accompany it. Its interest and value may be ephemeral even to those who find it amusing today. And so, to these I bid at last, *"Good fortune!"*

Endnotes

[i] Shakespeare, William. *Julius Caesar*, Act III, Scene 2.
[ii] Waite, Arthur Edward. **The Pictorial Key to the Tarot**. US Games Systems, Inc. Stamford CT, 1994. Originally published in 1910.
[iii] Kaplan, Stuart R. **The TAROT of the Witches Book**. US Games Systems, Inc. Stamford, CT, 1982. p. 18.
[iv] E.g., the scandal involving Rep. Mark Foley's **(R-FL)** inappropriate contacts with Congressional pages ("Page-gate"; see *Watergate* and *The Moon*) which burst unexpectedly on the nation just before midterm elections in Nov., 2006. Page-gate was the "last straw" for some Republican voters, contributing to Democrats' taking control of the US House of Representatives for the first time in 12 years.
[v] E.g., Skull & Bones, the Yale University secret society to which all of our most recent Presidents have belonged, or the Illuminati, or Tri-Lateral Commission, or World Banking Conspiracy...
[vi] Political analyst Ryan Sager titled his book about conflict between the Christian right and Libertarians for control of the Republican Party **The Elephant in the Room** (John Wiley & Sons, Inc., Hoboken, NJ, 2006), a play on the English idiom signifying a plain truth that is being ignored, and the Republican symbol.
[vii] Republican. http://www.urbandictionary.com/define.php?term=republican
[viii] Wikipedia contributors. **Elephant**. Wikipedia, The Free Encyclopedia. At: http://en.wikipedia.org/w/index.php?title=Elephant&oldid=156234301 (See also Danish Royal Order of the Elephant.)
[ix] Ibid.
[x] At one time this term might have been thought to refer to billionaire investor Donald Trump, who in 1999 formed a committee to assess his making a Presidential bid. Days later, Trump quit the Republican Party and joined **Ross Perot**'s Reform Party, saying that Republicans were "too crazy right." He was joined in making this switch, on the same day, by **Christian Right** leader **Pat Buchanan**. Center for Voting and Democracy, Major Events in U.S. Presidential Campaign 2000. http://www.fairvote.org/e_news/pres_campaign_events_2000.htm.

Since 2000, Trump's eccentricity, self-aggrandizing projects and "reality television" shows, and, most of all, his execrable taste in women, have made his assessment of Republicans as "too crazy" even more convincing. "The Donald" knows crazy!
[xi] Waite, op. cit. p. 15.
[xii] Ibid.
[xiii] *Time*, commonly called *Temperance*; and *Strength*, or *Fortitude*, are the others.
[xiv] A reference to President **Nixon**'s attempted evasion of responsibility for the *Watergate* scandal, of which much shall be said in these pages.

[xv] Waite, op. cit., p 24. Uncharacteristically, Waite, mis-spoke here. One of the earliest Tarot decks, the incomplete Charles VI or "Gringonneur" deck, shows *Prudence* in the 14th position, omitting *Temperance/Time* altogether. The essential element of a *missing virtue* remains! See Starbird, Margaret, **The Woman With the Alabaster Jar**. Bear & Company Publishing, Rochester, VT, 1993.

[xvi] Hoyle Pocket Trivia Game. Series 6, **Political Trivia**. Hoyle Products, St. Paul, MN, 1984.

[xvii] Ouspensky, P. D. The symbolism of the Tarot: philosophy of occultism in pictures and numbers. Translated by A. L. Pogossky. Trood Print. and Pub. Co. St. Petersburg, Russia. 1913. Scanned at www.sacred-texts.com, Dec. 2003, JB Hare, redacter. I am grateful to Ms. Braun for bringing it to my attention.

[xviii] Waite, op. cit., p. 26.

[xix] The Bell Telephone Company (at this writing, AT&T) has used various monikers as regulatory tides have waxed and waned, but its cultural significance was well-expressed in *The President's Analyst*, starring James Coburn (Paramount Pictures, 1967). We may also recall the proclivity of the 19th century yellow press to call any female criminal over the age of 25 "Ma".

[xx] Waite, op. cit., p. 29.

[xxi] Published by US Games Systems, Inc., Stamford, CT, 1982.

[xxii] A long-venerated symbol of prosperity, fertility, and cheap foreign labor; see, e.g., the South Seas epic of James Michener, **Hawaii** (Random House, 1959).

[xxiii] The observant reader will note a preponderance of African-Americans representing this suite, led by **Colin Powell** and **Condoleezza Rice**. This is neither an attempt to perpetuate segregation, nor to offend other ethnic and racial groups not well-represented herein, but to recognize the historic connection of Black Americans with the Republican Party. Modern Republicanism was founded to oppose slavery; this is what some term irony.

[xxiv] The question remains unanswered, *'What shall the husband of a woman President be called?'* **Mrs. Clinton** (US Senate, **D-NY**) aims to see it settled, but the matter is far from firm.

[xxv] A psychic act not unlike that of spontaneous combustion, *infra*, dig?

[xxvi] Sesame St., Transylvania, that is, employing alphabet cards, and number cards featuring *The* Count.

[xxvii] Cairo, Illinois.

[xxviii] See the works of scorned scientist Immanuel Velikovsky on why the Ancients considered Jupiter, which most modern Earthlings cannot find in the night sky, the ruler of the planet-Gods, and how Mars and Venus warred in the heavens over Troy. Our ancestors were far less foolish than we have been taught!

[xxix] Alexander Wallinsky-Nieves, a Welsh-Rumanian ski instructor, or "bum."

[xxx] Thanks and a tip of the Pointy-Headed Wizard's Cap, for reminding me of this historic use, to Donna Salm., "La Rosa de San Antonio". See Starbird, op. cit.

Oddly, on the same day Ms. Salm e-mailed me about Starbird's book, Ms. Braun e-mailed an offer to lend it. These ladies are not acquainted and do not reside in the same city. This is what the unenlightened call "coincidence"!

Waite dropped hints of the "Grail heresy" in terms so obscure and evasive as to defy even satire!

xxxi Gonick, Larry. **The Cartoon History of the United States**. Harper Perennial, New York, 1991, p. 114. The difference between **Jefferson**'s advocacy of **Term Limits** and that of later proponents is that the Master of Monticello had a life outside of politics, inventing agricultural tools, smoking cannabis hemp, and fathering children upon his Black slave-mistress; he showed no inclination to hang around and meddle with government in his sunset years.

xxxii In a letter to **Jefferson**'s Secretary of the Treasury, Albert Gallatin, quoted by Richard Hofstadter in **The American Political Tradition**. Alfred Knopf, Inc., New York, 1948. p. 45.

xxxiii Hoyle, op. cit.

xxxiv "Greedy On Principle"; "Grand Ol' Pedophiles", etc.

xxxv Gonick, op. cit., p. 167 *(italics derived from one of Gonick's drawings following quoted text)*.

xxxvi Including, apparently, not having the right not to be constantly imitated, and at the same time condescended to, by rhythmically impaired White people. You cannot sing the Blues in a waterfront condominium on Lake Tahoe, no matter how much jello you done shot in Memphis!

xxxvii As an attorney, **Lincoln** was naturally adept at speaking out of both sides of his mouth. He was known to make jokes at his own expense, and is thought to have originated the derogatory lawyer joke. (**Q**. *"How many lawyers does it take to defend a Confederate general?"* **A**. *"Three! One to tie the rope, one to slap the horse, and one to get the feller's wallet!"*)

xxxviii If there had been a Frontier Wrestling Federation, "Honest Abe" would have been a feared competitor.

xxxix Similar in intent to the meanly discriminatory "Jim Crow" laws of the post-World War II era. It has been theorized in late-night pot-smoking sessions that the greatest overlooked influences in eventually overcoming these latter-day insults were the beloved Crows, clearly based on stereotypical Southern Negroes, who befriended a sad baby **Elephant** in the animated Disney classic *Dumbo* (1941). Moreover, those birds gave millions of White toddlers throughout the '40s and '50s their first glimpse of *cool*.

xl It was about this time that advertising slogans were invented, as in, *"Find 'em, fool 'em, and void their warranty!!"*

xli Yes, Virginia, there was a time when Republicans found Darwin's doctrine of "survival of the fittest" useful; by the 1990s, even this nod to science had been squashed by the **Christian Right**. All that most people in the 1870s knew of evolution was that it somehow decreed the "survival of the fittest"; as in, *those that don't survive are not fit to do so*; e.g., if Native Americans died when exposed to smallpox-infected blankets, it was only because they were not "fit" to live.

xlii That is, a Democrat who opposed *Republican* corruption.

xliii Gonick, op. cit., p. 226

xliv Hofstadter, op. cit., p. 218.

xlv Hoyle, op. cit.

xlvi More than two Presidential terms for one individual were still permitted at that time. This was only forbidden with ratification of the 22nd Amendment in 1951, but the only President to serve more than two terms, even before the amendment was passed, was Democrat Franklin Roosevelt, elected four times.

[xlvii] Coffey, Thomas M. **The Long Thirst**. W. W. Norton & Company, Inc., New York, 1975. p. *x*. Italics added.

[xlviii] Ibid., p. *xi*. Note that the present volume is being published late in 2007, more than 40 years after Coffey's; need it be said that the problems he described have increased astronomically during this time?

[xlix] **Harding** was reportedly the first Senator to "bear the white flag" in surrendering to intense, coordinated public pressure from the Anti-Saloon League to pass the Volstead Amendment. Alcohol Problems and Solutions. **National Prohibiton of Alcohol in the U.S.** http://www2.potsdam.edu/hansondj/Controversies/1091124904_3.html.

The most amusing of the **Prohibition** Presidents, Harding was appalled to learn that the Act really meant that respectable gentlemen such as himself and his cronies might not enjoy a few companionable highballs ("elevenses"), and only publicly renounced Demon Rum after some two years in office.

[l] Known as "the Bald One" (Hoyle, op. cit.), and as "Silent Cal" (Webster, III, Orville V. **The Book of Presidents**. JBG Publishing, Los Angeles, 1991, p. 88).

[li] Some irresponsible historians blame the stock market crash of 1929, the Depression, and President Hoover's unpopularity all on **Prohibition**, positing that, had people been allowed to drink, they might not have been so depressed, and the economy wouldn't have collapsed. It does seem to be a fact that even in the worst of economic times, people find funds for their "vices", legal or not.

[lii] I shall, in this context, mention *en passant* an old superstition, doubtless containing no truth whatsoever, that a "used" tarot deck can bring "bad luck", in that it retains a psychic impression not only of its practitioner, *but of each seeker who has handled it*. There are only six degrees of separation between you and any other individual in the world, including those scary people who live under the bridge. Wash your hands well, and obtain fresh **Republican Tarot** cards often!

[liii] Webster, op. cit, p. 14.

[liv] Webster, op. cit., p. 63.

[lv] Wikipedia contributors. **James Garfield**. Wikipedia, The Free Encyclopedia. Available at: http://en.wikipedia.org/w/index.php?title=James_Garfield&oldid=138392361.

[lvi] Webster, op. cit., p. 67. Unfortunately, this technological capability was lost in a later renovation of the Oval Office, and thus unavailable to President **George W. Bush** when Hurricane Katrina struck the Gulf Coast city in 2005.

[lvii] Wikipedia contributors. **Chester A. Arthur**. Wikipedia, The Free Encyclopedia. Available at: http://en.wikipedia.org/w/index.php?title=Chester_A._Arthur&oldid=138129145.

[lviii] Wikipedia contributors. **Chester A. Arthur**. Wikipedia, The Free Encyclopedia. Available at: http://en.wikipedia.org/w/index.php?title=Chester_A._Arthur&oldid=158975335

[lix] Webster, op. cit., p. 71.

[lx] Wikipedia contributors. **Benjamin Harrison**. Wikipedia, The Free Encyclopedia. Available at:

http://en.wikipedia.org/w/index.php?title=Benjamin_Harrison&oldid=137714206.
lxi Webster, op. cit., p. 75.
lxii Wikipedia contributors. **William Howard Taft**. Wikipedia, The Free Encyclopedia. Available at: http://en.wikipedia.org/w/index.php?title=William_Howard_Taft&oldid=138333690.
lxiii Hoyle, op. cit.
lxiv Webster, op. cit., p. 76-78.
lxv Webster, op. cit., p. 90-91.
lxvi Hoyle, op. cit.
lxvii Bass, Jack, and Marilyn W. Thompson. **'Ol' Strom: An Unauthorized Biography of Strom Thurmond**. University of South Carolina Press, 2003.
lxviii Webster, op. cit., p. 101.
lxix Hoyle, op. cit.
lxx Hoyle, op. cit.
lxxi Webster, op. cit., p. 115.
lxxii Webster, op. cit., p. 127-128.
lxxiii Half-baked assertions have been overheard while inebriated, at half-remembered parties in since-demolished buildings, that young **George W.** was a mediocre student in Austin in 1964-65, barely passing required freshman English, which most English-speaking students "place out of" (do not have to take) by passing a written test; also, that someone strongly resembling the future President and his bosom companions tried to assault an offensively "long-haired hippie" once upon an evening, causing the startled fellow to reflexively heft an axe kept for wood-chopping purposes; no records remain; denial reigns.
lxxiv See **Oliver North**, *IX of Bushes*.
lxxv Wikipedia contributors. **Iran hostage crisis**. Wikipedia, The Free Encyclopedia. Available at: http://en.wikipedia.org/w/index.php?title=Iran_hostage_crisis&oldid=155591512.
lxxvi Wikipedia contributors. **Gerald Ford**. Wikipedia, The Free Encyclopedia. Available at: http://en.wikipedia.org/w/index.php?title=Gerald_Ford&oldid=138295083.
lxxvii Hoyle, op. cit.
lxxviii The dog star, not Disney's star dog.
lxxix Ms. Kate Braun, in correspondence with the author, Jan. 5, 1996.
lxxx Wikipedia contributors. **Martha Beall Mitchell**. Wikipedia, The Free Encyclopedia. Available at: http://en.wikipedia.org/w/index.php?title=Martha_Beall_Mitchell&oldid=122160619.
lxxxi Kammerman, Roy. **Poor Richard's WATERGATE**. Price/Stern/Sloan, Publishers, Inc., Los Angeles, CA. 1973.
lxxxii Wikipedia contributors. **John N. Mitchell**. Wikipedia, The Free Encyclopedia. Available at: http://en.wikipedia.org/w/index.php?title=John_N._Mitchell&oldid=138601187.

lxxxiii Unlike the Doggone people, **Lincoln** would hardly have killed and eaten his visitors without first determining whether they had any legal issues which might require his services!

lxxxiv **Lincoln** remains the tallest President to date, although the average height of US residents has increased substantially since his day. Hoyle, op. cit.

lxxxv Garson, Barbara. Grove Press, 1967.

lxxxvi A term popularized by **Rush Limbaugh**.

lxxxvii Hoyle, op. cit.

lxxxviii Wikipedia contributors. **Henry Kissinger**. Wikipedia, The Free Encyclopedia. Available at: http://en.wikipedia.org/w/index.php?title=Henry_Kissinger&oldid=136959691

lxxxix Waite, op. cit., p. 124.

xc Ouspensky, op. cit.

xci It may be noted that the 8-fold path, or 8-spoked "Wheel of Law", Dharmachakra, figures prominently in Eastern philosophies; no conclusions need be drawn.

lxvii In a zodiacal aside, Mars was the planet originally associated with Aquarius. Modern astrologers place Uranus there. The naked female in the illustration seems to be showing us hers!

xciii To get a true understanding of the scope of the problem, and if you can stomach it, see The "Family Values" People, http://www.republicansexoffenders.com.

xciv On Aug. 28, 2007, as I was finishing this manuscript, US Senator Larry Craig **(R-ID)**, leading Republican on several Senate committees, admitted pleading guilty to soliciting lewd behavior in an airport men's room and hiding his arrest from his family and the public for 77 days. While disinclined to re-order my pages to afford this fool more than a footnote, let it be noted that his misadventure *immediately* diverted the fickle **Media**'s attention from Aug. 27th's resignation by US Attorney General Alberto Gonzales, the Architect of torture at Abu Ghraib prison, secret wiretapping of American citizens under the guise of the so-called "Patriot Act", and politically-motivated firings of Assistant US Attorney Generals. Yes, Larry, "you def'nit'ly da 'ho!"

   ADDENDUM: Not a month later, yet another high-ranking Republican has been charged with pedophilia. The mind reels; the stomach lurches. We recall once again the periodic *musth*-induced transgressions of elephants.

xcv Wikipedia contributors. **Newt Gingrich**. Wikipedia, The Free Encyclopedia. Available at: http://en.wikipedia.org/w/index.php?title=Newt_Gingrich&oldid=139050372.

xcvi Ed Mierzwinski of the US Public Interest Research Group, quoted by Rugaber, Christopher S. **Court**'s ideological split largely absent in business cases. Associated Press. July 1, 2007.

xcvii Waite, op. cit., p. 148.

xcviii Wikipedia contributors. **Ross Perot**. Wikipedia, The Free Encyclopedia. Available at: http://en.wikipedia.org/w/index.php?title=Ross_Perot&oldid=139044234.

xcix **G.H.W. Bush**'s brother, Prescott Bush, Jr., owned the only company allowed to do business with China during the US embargo of the Communist nation, exporting communications satellites. Prescott Jr. retired as Chairman of the USA-China Chamber of Commerce in 2006. Here In Reality.com. **Bush Family Values Photo Album**. Available at: http://www.hereinreality.com/familyvalyes.html.

c Prescott Bush, Sr.. owned companies seized during World War II under the Trading with the Enemy Act, because they were fronts for Nazi industrialist Fritz Thyssen, a major financier of the Third Reich. Ibid.

ci Bentsen would later be the Democratic nominee for Vice President, on a ticket with Massachusetts Governor Michael Dukakis, losing to **Bush I**.

cii Later, FBI and CIA documents revealed that his oil company, Zapata Petroleum, began when he collaborated with CIA officer Thomas Devine in the 1950's. Devine would go with **Bush** to Vietnam as a CIA asset, act as his informal foreign affairs advisor, and remain close through 1975. Wikipedia contributors. **Zapata Corporation**. Wikipedia, The Free Encyclopedia. Available at: http://en.wikipedia.org/w/index.php?title=Zapata_Corporation&oldid=154481872.

ciii This expedition, the largest American military operation since Vietnam to that date, was directed by Joint Chiefs of Staff Chairman General **Colin Powell** who — as National Security Advisor for **Reagan** — knew Panama well. Wikipedia contributors. **Colin Powell**. Wikipedia, The Free Encyclopedia. Available at: http://en.wikipedia.org/w/index.php?title=Colin_Powell&oldid=156505327

civ Wikipedia contributors. **George H. W. Bush**. Wikipedia, The Free Encyclopedia. Available at: http://en.wikipedia.org/w/index.php?title=George_H._W._Bush&oldid=140229357.

cv About.com: Women's History. **Barbara Bush**. Available at: http://womenshistory.about.com/od/1stlady/bush1/p/barbara_bush.htm.

cvi Nichols, John. Barbara Bush: It's good enough for the poor. *The Nation Blog*, "The Online Beat". Posted Sept. 6, 2005. Available at: http://www.thenation.com/blogs/thebeat?pid=20080.

cvii Wikipedia contributors. **Barbara Bush**. Wikipedia, The Free Encyclopedia. Available at: http://en.wikipedia.org/w/index.php?title=Barbara_Bush&oldid=141867361.

cviii Wikipedia contributors. **George W. Bush**. Wikipedia, The Free Encyclopedia. Available at: http://en.wikipedia.org/w/index.php?title=George_W._Bush&oldid=142330915.

cix See brother **Neil Bush**, below.

cx Wikipedia, **George W. Bush**, op. cit.

cxi About.com., **Barbara Bush**, op. cit.

cxii Wikipedia contributors. **Jeb Bush**. Wikipedia, The Free Encyclopedia. Available at: http://en.wikipedia.org/w/index.php?title=Jeb_Bush&oldid=141497999.

cxiii Columba tried to smuggle almost $20,000 worth of clothes and jewelry into the US without paying import taxes on them after a vacation in France. Here In Reality.com, **Bush Family** Values Photo Album, op. cit.

cxiv Royce K, Brune T. Neil Bush, Ratzinger co-founders. *Newsday*, Washington Bureau. April 21, 2005. Available at:

http://www.newsday.com/news/nationworld/world/ny-wochar214226829apr21,0,106837.
[cxv] Associated Press Domestic News. March 31, 1981. Available at: http://www.hereinreality.com/hinckley.html.
[cxvi] Wikipedia contributors. **Oliver North**. Wikipedia, The Free Encyclopedia. Available at: http://en.wikipedia.org/w/index.php?title=Oliver_North&oldid=141745606.
[cxvii] *The Oregonian*. Broadcast Briefs. August 6, 1996.
[cxviii] National Organization for the Reform of Marijuana Laws (NORML). http://www.norml.org
[cxix] NORML, Ibid.
[cxx] *Frontline*. Dangerous prescription: The FDA: Hazardous to your health? http://www.pbs.org/wgbh/pages/frontline/shows/prescription/hazard
[cxxi] Angell, Marcia. The truth about the drug companies. *The New York Review of Books*. July 15, 2004;51(12). Available at: http://www.nybooks.com/articles/17244
[cxxii] Solomon, Norman. The power and glory of the **Heritage Foundation**. *The Oregon PeaceWorker*, Salem, OR, June, 1996.
[cxxiii] See **Christian Right**, *Six of Bushes*.
[cxxiv] See Iran-Contra affair discussion in *Trump IV, The Emperor*; the *Player of Bushes*; and the *Nine of Bushes*.
[cxxv] **Buchanan** calls the culture war a conflict over the power to define right and wrong. Fronts include environmentalism, feminism, **Abortion**, **Gay** rights, freedom of **Religion**, **Women** in combat, display of the Confederate Flag, the vicious "war on Christmas", taxpayer-funded art and more.
[cxxvi] Wikipedia contributors. **Pat Buchanan**. Wikipedia, The Free Encyclopedia. Available at: http://en.wikipedia.org/w/index.php?title=Pat_Buchanan&oldid=146245302.
[cxxvii] From the official website of the **Log Cabin Republicans**, http://online.logcabin.org/about.
[cxxviii] **Democrats.com, Gay Republicans**. http://blog.democrats.com/gayrepublicans.
[cxxix] The wisdom of **Ann Coulter**. *Washington Monthly Online*. October 2001. Available at: http://www.washingtonmonthly.com/features/2001/0111.coultrwisdom.html.
[cxxx] Wikipedia contributors. **Ann Coulter**. Wikipedia, The Free Encyclopedia. Available at: http://en.wikipedia.org/w/index.php?title=Ann_Coulter&oldid=141323811
[cxxxi] **Sony Bono** biography. http://mama.essortment.com/sonnybonobiogr_rqsb.htm
[cxxxii] **Cher** biography. http://www.sing365.com/music/lyric.nsf/Cher-Biography/36D174CAA94AC643482568730010A2DE
[cxxxiii] Wikipedia contributors. **Dan Quayle**. Wikipedia, The Free Encyclopedia. Available at: http://en.wikipedia.org/w/index.php?title=Dan_Quayle&oldid=142715423.

cxxxiv Wikipedia contributors. **Warren G. Harding**. Wikipedia, The Free Encyclopedia. Available at: http://en.wikipedia.org/w/index.php?title=Warren_G._Harding&oldid=143604757.
cxxxv Coffey, Thomas M., op. cit.
cxxxvi See **Oliver North**, *Nine of Bushes*.
cxxxvii Wikipedia contributors. **Colin Powell**. Wikipedia, op. cit.
cxxxviii Packer, George. Best. Staff. Officer. Ever. *Washington Post*, reprinted in the *Austin American-Statesman*, Feb. 25, 2007. Packer, a *Post* staffer, reviews colleague Karen DeYoung's biography, **Soldier: The life of Colin Powell**, Knopf, 2006.
cxxxix Ibid.
cxl Wikipedia contributors. **Condoleezza Rice**. Wikipedia, The Free Encyclopedia. Available at: http://en.wikipedia.org/w/index.php?title=Condoleezza_Rice&oldid=154836241.
cxli Wikipedia contributors. **Clarence Thomas**. Wikipedia, The Free Encyclopedia. Available at: http://en.wikipedia.org/w/index.php?title=Clarence_Thomas&oldid=151158418.
cxlii Having placed an emphasis in this suite on Black Americans, as stated above, in recognition of the special relationship which has obtained between them and the Party of which I write, I must here point out the derogatory nature of the terms "blacklist" and "blackmail"; just two of many negative and even ominous terms sustained by White guilt and fear of wronged Blackness. While such terms may seem today to be free of racial content, I predict a day when they, and similar words and phrases, will be as obsolete as the obscenely segregated public drinking fountains and restrooms of my childhood.
cxliii Wikipedia contributors. **Joseph McCarthy**. Wikipedia, The Free Encyclopedia. Available at: http://en.wikipedia.org/w/index.php?title=Joseph_McCarthy&oldid=155004341
cxliv http://veterans.house.gov/hearings/Testimony.aspx?TID=5226
cxlv Gates, Anita. **Tammy Faye Bakker**, 56, emotive evangelist, dies. *The New York Times*, July 22, 2007.
cxlvi Ibid.
cxlvii Hartsoe, Steve. Televangelist known for makeup, ministry. Associated Press. Carried in the *Austin American-Statesman*, July 22, 2007.
cxlviii Gates, op. cit. Do note the name of the play! Nothing could be more apt!
cxlix Phyllis Schafley was a vocal and abrasive leader of anti-abortion forces.
cl The youngest man yet sworn in as President, including John F. Kennedy, who most folks believe was the youngest -- perhaps your friends may bet on it!
cli Hoyle, op. cit.
clii Wikipedia contributors. **James Meredith**. Wikipedia, The Free Encyclopedia. Available at: http://en.wikipedia.org/w/index.php?title=James_Meredith&oldid=151232756.
cliii Ibid.

[cliv] Although not the first to go down in a sub; see note LXIV above.
[clv] Hoyle, op. cit.
[clvi] Waite. op. cit., p. 252.

[clvii] During the Civil War, a picture of **Grant** with a cigar appeared. He was swamped with cigars from well wishers. Before, he had smoked only sporadically, but he couldn't give them all away, so he started smoking them; one claim is he smoked over 10,000 in five years.

[clviii] Wikipedia contributors. **Ulysses S. Grant**. Wikipedia, The Free Encyclopedia. Available at: http://en.wikipedia.org/w/index.php?title=Ulysses_S._Grant&oldid=144078767.

[clix] Hoyle, op. cit.

[clx] Wikipedia contributors. **Kay Bailey Hutchison**. Wikipedia, The Free Encyclopedia. Available at: http://en.wikipedia.org/w/index.php?title=Kay_Bailey_Hutchison&oldid=143807404

[clxi] Waters, Roger. "Another Brick in the Wall, Part II (We don't need no education)", from Pink Floyd's *The Wall*, 1979.

[clxii] Thanks and a tip of the Wizard cap to Mark Kleiman, Esq., Los Angeles, CA.

[clxiii] Thanks for the metaphor, and greetings, to Timbuk 3, wherever you are.

[clxiv] Surely it may be granted by the generous Reader, who has already granted so much, that despite the surface similarity of his name, the Englishman John Maynard Keynes, architect of tax-and-spend liberal economics, may be fairly excluded from consideration here, even though **Richard Nixon** is reported to have said, in 1971, "*We are all Keynesians now.*" See Lozada C. The economics of dirty dishes. *Washington Post*. Aug. 5, 2007.

[clxv] Francis Scott **Key**. http://www.francisscottkey.org

[clxvi] Wikipedia contributors. **Alan Keyes**. Wikipedia, The Free Encyclopedia. Available at: http://en.wikipedia.org/w/index.php?title=Alan_Keyes&oldid=137805708.

[clxvii] Skane, Neil. Trojan donkey? Republicans make nice, Dems love it, but is all what it seems? *Florida Trend*. April 1, 2007.

[clxviii] In the July 7, 2007 episode of the popular comic strip.

[clxix] Or "Shrub", as our dear departed Molly Ivins dubbed the former Governor of Texas.

[clxx] Look for my next book!

[clxxi] An internet-derived word indicating use of the "Google" search engine. This word has entered the popular lexicon despite the opposition of its corporate owners, who wish to protect its copyright. At present, it is unclear whether use of the verb "to google" will be ruled an infringement of which every computer user on Earth is guilty, or a case of success, as we have seen so often within these pages, begetting the seeds of its own destruction.

[clxxii] What Pulitzer Prize-winning American author Michael Chabon calls, in **Wonder Boys** (Fourth Estate Limited, London, 1995), "the midnight disease".

Praise for SIXTY:

"I recently received a copy of a new book of photographs and poems written by two people who have been friends for thirty years. Mariann Wizard and Scout Stormcloud have put their skills together to produce **SIXTY**, a collection of Mariann's poetry and Scout's photographs. This collection is a delightful collage for the eyes and for the soul. It drew me in and keeps me coming back to see what other insights are hidden within.

"Lying in amongst the beautiful flowers, the poems range from the personal 'Night a Trois', or 'The Kind of Man I'm Drawn To', to the political as in 'The Last Spring,' or 'The Real Dragon,' about political prisoner Marilyn Buck."

— **Robert Pardun**, author of **Prairie Radical**

"A few of the poems are as steamy as a late May afternoon after a thunderstorm. All of them, from traditional verse to haiku, invite reading and reflection."

— **Mike Cox**, author of **Texas Ranger Tales, Vols. I & II** and **Texas Disasters: True Stories of Tragedy and Survival**; Texana reviewer, in **Lone Star Book Blog**, http://lonestarbooks.blogspot.com/2007/05/wizardry-writing.html

"Scout's photos made me homesick for Texas. I wished I was sitting in the back yard (of my parents' home) in Austin, sipping on a gin and tonic."

— **Marilyn Buck**, author of **Rescue the Word**, the **Red Poppies** CD, and other poems

"Wise & whimsical & whizzing forward through eras & landscapes at **SIXTY**, poet Wizard & photographer Stormcloud took me for a scenic ride into deep places I recognize but never quite saw the way they show, singing as we go."

— Northern California radio personality "**Latenight Liz**" Helenchild

"Mariann is still changing the world, this time with her poetry. The words flow, and the selection of Scout Stormcloud's photographs... is perfect. A book with built-in *feng shui*. This is a book to read to your children, your lover, or to yourself. It will move any who partake of its riches. Be sure to hear Mariann's poetry put to music on her Web site. You will understand even more fully the human-ness of her words. Mariann and Scout are two remarkable women, two wonderful artists."

— **Richard Jehn**, author of **Feasting with Family and Friends**

"[A] mature vision for a generation that still has yet to fully resolve issues that came to us along our way. I was struck first by love poems that came off the page like langorous deep soul pillowtalk... an out of body experience of the mind of the other, quite sexy. She deals with the great experience of our time, Vietnam... and the radical rebel experiences of subversive free thought... Doesn't pull punches, but lovingly so. I find myself wanting... more of this pillowtalk...."

— **Stuart Heady**, poet, essayist, and artist

Order **S I X T Y** from Lulu.com, Barnes &Noble.com, Amazon.com, or Borders.com. Print-on-demand and electronic versions are available.

Ask your favorite bookstore to order **S I X T Y** for you, and for other folks who enjoy beautiful full-color photography and powerful, straightforward, accessible poems & songs! Hear some of My Music at:

A Wizard's Life   http://awizardslife.com

THE REPUBLICAN TAROT

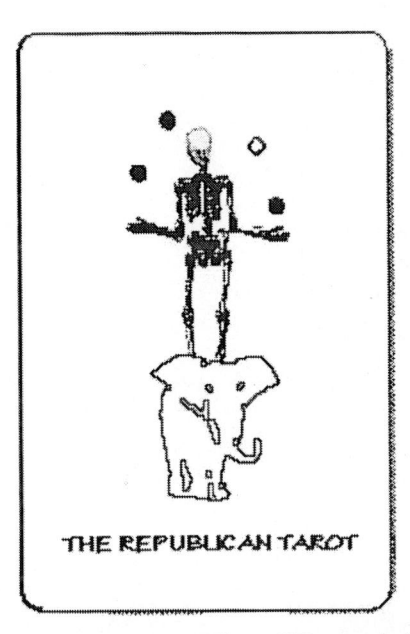

Thanks for purchasing **The Pictorial Key to the Republican Tarot!** If you don't yet have the **Electronic Republican Tarot Deck*** (**see photo opposite**), you can download it for FREE from:

http://stores.lulu.com/mgwizard!

Double the fun of **The Republican Tarot** with a *Full-Color, 80-card* Deck you can print and assemble yourself, using common office supplies and 5th grade skills! Deck includes its own sturdy Box and handy 32-page reference booklet, **Introduction to the Republican Tarot!** Bonus Cards, Postcards, more!

History – Humor – and a Perfectly Good Deck of Cards! Download your *Major Party Fun* today!

* © Mariann G. Wizard, All Rights Reserved
ESN 91412-070918-831261-62
registered at http://numly.com